GW00361731

MORE CRICKET EXTRAS

DAVID RAYVERN ALLEN

Illustrations by
David Arthur

GUINNESS PUBLISHING

Copyright © David Rayvern Allen 1992
Reprinted 1994

The right of David Rayvern Allen to be identified as the Author of this Work has
been asserted in accordance with the Copyright, Design & Patents Act 1988.

Published in Great Britain by Guinness Publishing Ltd,
33 London Road, Enfield, Middlesex

'Our Constitution . . .' (page 23) first published in, and reproduced by kind
permission of, The Journal of the Cricket Society.
'Limestone' (page 124) first published in 1986 by Littlewood Press, reproduced
by kind permission of the author.

Illustrations by David Arthur

Designed by Kathleen Aldridge

Typeset in Palatino by Ace Filmsetting Ltd, Frome, Somerset

Printed and bound in Great Britain by The Bath Press, Bath

'Guinness' is a registered trademark of Guinness Publishing Ltd

A catalogue record for this book is available from the British Library.

ISBN 0–85112–534–4

CONTENTS

THE AUTHOR

Cricket writer, musician and award-winning radio
producer, David Rayvern Allen has also shown
himself to be a fine accumulator of Cricket Extras –
this book is his second collection of those weird and
wonderful tales from on and off the field.

A lifetime's involvement with music began with
David distinguishing himself during National Service
by dropping cymbals on parade grounds. He moved
on to playing the piano in theatre musicals and it was
while playing in a production called *This Way to the
Tomb* that it occurred to David, as he says, that it
might be a good idea to join BBC Television!

He spent four years in television involved in the
musical content of everything from opera to old-style
variety. Since then he has worked as a producer for all

the networks on BBC Radio in a successful career which has seen him win many awards – most recently and most notably the Prix Monte Carlo and Prix Italia (1991) for *Who Pays the Piper* – and receive six Sony nominations.

His many published cricket writings include *A Song for Cricket, Cricket on the Air* and several anthologies of John Arlott's broadcasts and writings. He has also contributed to *The Cricketer* and *Wisden Cricket Monthly*. That is not to say that his playing career has been without distinction – David firmly believes he must be the only person ever to be bowled first ball by a nonagenarian in the nets at the Hollywood Cricket Club!

The author would like to extend special thanks to the following for their help in preparing *More Cricket Extras*: Geoffrey Copinger, Simon Duncan, David Frith, Stephen Green, Bunty Ireland, Evelyn James, Pauline Jones, Derek Lodge, Charles Richards and Glenys Williams. Every effort has been made to trace copyright holders of material reproduced in *More Cricket Extras* – any overlooked are invited to contact the author.

CRICKET IN FOREIGN FIELDS

Where lie cricket's roots?
Anybody seeking the answer in the 14 000 or so books on cricket might be taken on a round trip through Northern France, Denmark, Germany, Holland to Persia, Ancient Egypt and Lydia. On the other hand, they might be dropped closer to home in the Kentish Weald and on Hampshire Down. The truth is that nobody can be sure where any pastime started that evolved from hitting a round object with a piece of wood. Nor does it really matter.

What we can be sure of is that wherever pink coloured the map of the world, there was cricket. The Army, the Navy, missionaries and those working for the British Government were largely responsible. A line from an article in *Blackwood's Edinburgh Magazine* of 1892 puts it succinctly: 'The Englishman carries his cricket bat with him as naturally as his gun case or his India rubber bath.' However, even if they were the catalysts, it was not only expat John Bulls who were aiming shooters at a wet patch from twenty-two yards.

And there lies the fascination. For cricket has found a crease in some fairly unlikely corners during the last two hundred years or so. As in so much of history, nobody can be absolutely certain of the exact dates when stumps were first placed in different parts of the world; all that can be said is that by such and such a time the game was known to have appeared at this or that place. Mind you, the gazetteer that follows does not necessarily include the first known entry, rather some early references and random reflections of cricket's geographical spread:

1709 Receiver-General, William Byrd, playing cricket by St James River, Virginia.

1721 Seamen of the East India Company playing cricket at Cambay, India.

1725 Cricket known to have been played at Boston, New England.

1736 The crews of HM ships at Lisbon playing cricket in the city.

1737 Mention of the game in Georgia, USA.

1741 Cricket played on Christmas Day at Savannah, Georgia.

1747 Cricket played in New York, formerly New Amsterdam.

1751 A match in New York between New York and a London XI 'played according to the London method' (the 1744 Code).

1754 Cricket in Maryland.

c **1767** Cricket in Connecticut.

1780 Recently discovered belt buckle points to cricket in Barbados.

1785 French Canadians playing on Sundays in Montreal at the Ste-Helene.

1792 Calcutta CC known to exist.

1799 A club formed in southern India at Seringapatum.

1804 *Sydney Gazette* reports a month of cricket on Phillips Common.

1806 Meeting of St Anne's CC, Barbados.

1808 Capetown, South Africa. Game between Colony and Artillery Mess Officers.

1810 Match at Green Point Common in Capetown.

'He only wants to play!'

1818 The game is played at Valparaiso in Chile.
1819 Cricket played at Kingston, Ontario.
1832 First club formed in Ceylon.
1838 Club in Mexico City. Later teams included Pachuea, Velasco, Reforma, Monterrey and Rancheros of Muzquiz.
1839 Cricket in Kabul, Afghanistan.

Philip Snow has described how Bishop Wilson of Micronesia, playing in **New Britain** in the Solomon Islands, put himself on to bowl in the hope of capturing the vital wicket before the opposing side scored the runs needed. Snow noted how 'the spectators, including thin bush dogs and long-eared razor-backed pigs, all liked to make their presence felt . . . His first ball was hit into the sea. Onlookers shouted to the last pair batting to run. Wilson shouted to the fielders wading in the sea (which was too close to represent a boundary) to fling the ball in . . . The village dogs felt it imperative to take part. One in particular was unable to contain himself and as Wilson stood poised at the wicket to intercept the ball for the certain run-out that would bring his side victory, he seized the Rt Rev's rear to effect a quite different result.'

> *The Maharajah happened to mention to the visiting Test cricketer that his harem contained 298 wives. 'Hm,' grunted the cricketer, 'two more and you qualify for a new ball.'*

A guest player for Negri Sembilan, **Malaysia**, was Petero Kubunavanua who toured New Zealand in the 1948 Fiji team. During one match, he found

Kubunavanua's
Revenge . . .

himself stationed at deep square-leg on the shadowy side of the ground continually encircled by swallows. In the end, Kubunavanua could endure the distraction no longer; with a sudden sweep he plucked one out of the air and put it in his *sulu* (calf-length skirt) pocket.

Papua New Guinea, where cricket was introduced by missionaries towards the end of the nineteenth century as an alternative to head-hunting, have performed increasingly well in the ICC tournaments. In 1982 they surprisingly beat Canada.

Fijians are effervescent cricketers whether they are 'cutting, driving, hooking, throwing, catching or bowling with all their might'. A number of times they have achieved surprising results against national sides that on paper have seemed far stronger. Perhaps the bare feet, flying *sulus* and large heads of bristly hair have helped confer an outward ferocity that inhibits their opponents.

In 1942, Fiji dismissed a New Zealand Forces XI, including seven Plunket Shield players, for 25 in one innings. Shortly after this, one of Fiji's outstanding cricketers in this match, Turaga, was accidentally electrocuted at the Gold Mines.

B Kwong Wo, son of the groundsman at Chater Road, **Hong Kong**, is one of few Chinese to have played representative cricket. The ground, now lost to development, was surrounded by two skyscraper banks, the Supreme Court and the Hong Kong Hilton. In 1970, against an MCC side led by Tony Lewis, Kwong Wo spun out four batsmen, hit the highest score and fielded superbly.

Cricket was being played in **Nepal** in 1928 with two teams: one patronised by General Brahma SJB Rana of Babar Mahal, who scored the first century in the country six years later, and the other by General Nara SJB Rana in Jawalakhel.

By 1935, a cousin of General Brahma, General Madon, had become so addicted to the game that he had lured cricket coaches from Calcutta in India and constructed a small stadium in his palace 'Sri Durbar'.

According to the President of the Nepalese Cricket Association, Jai Kumar Nath Shah, cricket is extremely popular at present with more than 25 teams participating in various tournaments in Kathmandu alone. In 1989 at Biratnagar, a town in the Eastern Region, an Invitation Cup final was watched by 15000 people.

As a young boy, together with eight brothers, King Thebaw of **Burma** attended school in Mandalay. It was there that Dr Marles, a well-known missionary, taught him to bat, although he was 'in the habit of using very injurious language to anyone who bowled him'.

Two teams contest the South Atlantic Ocean Championship in **Tristan da Cunha**. They play on matting-covered concrete.

In West Africa, **Nigeria**, **The Gambia**, **Ghana** and **Sierra Leone** regularly play each other – there is also a league in Liberia. The Sierra Leone player with the highest profile has been the aggressively-named West Indian bowler, Stalin Adolf Fraser.

During the last few years, Asian Cup competitions and other cricket has taken place in a specially built huge stadium in the emirate of **Sharjah** due to the enthusiastic support of the wealthy Abdul Rehman Bukhatir, son of an Arab sheikh.

A sinister change of bowling in West Africa

Combining the duties of Umpire and Empire in Brazil

An early ground of **Rio** Cricket Club was in the Rua Paysandu, at the foot of a stone quarry. A constant visitor to the matches was the Emperor of Brazil, Don Pedro II.

Guatemala proposed to send a team to British Honduras in 1909, one year after Isaiah Thomas had issued a pamphlet in **Belize** entitled *A Concise Hint and Guide to Cricket*.

The Valley of Peace Cricket Club outside Christchurch, **New Zealand**, is a male bastion. 'We simply don't let women on the premises at all,' they say. 'No wives, fiancées, mistresses, or even barmaids or waitresses. That's why it's called The Valley of Peace.' When asked what they would do if the Queen called, they replied: 'We'd stop the game and go down to the gate to say hello.'

The touring Australians were smuggled out of the ground to escape the wrath of an angry crowd after a drawn game against **Philadelphia** in 1878.

Dave Gregory, the Australian captain, had taken his side off the field in protest after a disputed umpire's decision and only returned when threatened with the stoppage of the gate money. The time lost precluded a finish to a match that appeared to be going Philadelphia's way.

August 1885: **Spitzbergen**. HMS *Active* and *Calypso* v HMS *Volage* and *Ruby*. Played on the shores of Recherche Bay, Spitzbergen. The ground was a most picturesque one, being surrounded by glaciers. These latter are continually breaking up as they work

'We are not admitted – or amused!'

down into the sea, and the bay was thus studded with floating masses of ice, which added to the scenic effect. Play commenced late in the evening, and was continued till past midnight. In this latitude (77°30 N) cricket might be played all night through at this time of the year, the climate being warm enough (except when the wind is from the north). The match resulted in a win for HMS *Active* and *Calypso*.

(*The Field*)

Off-spinner Ashraful Gul, with 7 for 23 against Fiji in 1979, has produced the outstanding bowling performance for **Bangladesh** in international competition.

Kuwait Wanderers have toured India, Pakistan and Bahrain under the leadership of Chatrapal Sinh, a nephew of Duleepsinhji and a grand-nephew of Ranjitsinhji.

In **Norfolk Island** in the South Seas, there is an annual match, 'All Comers' v '*The Bounty*'.

> Conrad Hunte, West Indian cricket coach, advising young black South Africans on their future: 'Learn to dream.'

Samoa: Matches of two hundred a side took place (obviously MCC rules had to be liberally adapted) and lasted for weeks. It became the norm to have three batsmen

at each end and four or five umpires. Work in the fields was readily neglected and punitive measures had to be taken. Some who played were expelled from the Church, and the King (in the best pantomime tradition) issued a decree:

THE LAW REGARDING CRICKET

To all the Districts of Samoa, Notice
1 It is strictly prohibited for a village to travel and play cricket with another village.
2 It is strictly prohibited for two villages to play cricket together.
3 It is also prohibited for a village to play cricket among themselves.
4 Should any village or district fail to keep this law in any respect, they will be fined a sum not exceeding forty-five dollars, or in default be sent to jail for three months with hard labour.

MALIETOA,
The King of Samoa
Residence of the King, Apia
June 20, 1890

In time, a more reasonable and relaxed state of affairs prevailed, a Cricket Association was formed in 1916 and in 1992 a Samoan, Murphy Sua, a left-arm, fast-medium bowler and a lusty striker with the bat, gained a regular place in the New Zealand Test side.

In 1846, during a match between the **USA** and **Canada** in New York the Canadians were sliding towards defeat. In their second innings a batsman 'hit a ball back to the bowler and seeing that the bowler was about to catch it, charged the bowler down. The bowler successfully held the catch but, justifiably incensed, hurled the ball at the batsman, giving him a sharp blow on the thigh. The batsman was given out by the umpire but the other Canadian batsman went off the field with him. After some time, when no Canadian appeared, the umpires awarded the match to the Americans.'

Afterwards, the headstrong batsman claimed that he was acting within the laws!

By 1985 there had been 88 cricket tours to and from **Argentina** over 117 years. The first was to **Uruguay** in 1868.

The original minute book of the Orotava Cricket Club, Tenerife, **Canary Islands**, for the years 1826 and 1827 reveals that the Club had its own doctor and *apothecary*.

In March 1823, the crews of HM ships *Fury* and *Hecla*, clad in furs, played cricket close to the 70th parallel at **Igloolik**. It could have led to an original method of dismissal, 'frozen out'.

During the last century British sailors were not deterred from playing cricket by unsuitable terrain. They once took the trouble to clean an overgrown ditch surrounding an obsolete fortress in **Cyprus** for a pick-up match and on another occasion laid down boat sails on the edge of the **Sahara** to construct a makeshift 'square' amidst the dunes.

George Tubow II of **Tonga**, who died in 1918, was described as 'the last of the independent kings of the Pacific'. Tubow's attachment to cricket stemmed from schooldays in Auckland, New Zealand. His enthusiasm proved so infectious that many of his subjects devoted all their time to the game instead of working on the plantations and, as in Samoa, it became necessary to introduce restrictions. In order to avert famine, cricket was forbidden on weekdays.

Geoffrey Boycott and Alan Jones both scored centuries for MCC v Royal **Bangkok** Sports Club in 1970.

St Helena: Cricket grounds on the Racecourse at Deadwood, Longwood and Francis Plain near Jamestown, the capital. It is recorded that a cricket bat was in existence in Brighton some seventy years ago that had been 'made from a willow tree raised from a cutting taken by Mr Borrer from a tree by Napoleon's grave in 1840'.

Sumatra (Ashley-Cooper): 'The first match played at Madan Deli was between Langkat and Serdang. A Dutchman named Verhulst took 15 wickets for 38 runs for Serdang' in the two innings.

The cricketing Abrahams of **Israel** were able to field an all-family team.

During the 1960s, there was a pioneering tour of **Ethiopia** by Australian schoolboy cricketers.

The first game of organised cricket in **Japan** was probably Yokohama v Fleet in 1863. Eight years later, a teacher of English and French at Yonegawa English School, 'chaaresu henry darasu' – one interpretation is Charles Henry Dallas – taught his pupils the rudiments of the game.

EUROPEAN CONNECTIONS

It may be thought that the mainland of Europe has been an arid desert for cricket. Not entirely true, for the game does have a distinctive countenance in Holland and Denmark and a new European tournament took place in 1992.

Perhaps very soon, it may no longer be possible to agree with John Board when he wrote: 'Apparently the game fails to appeal to the Latin, the Teuton or the Slav. It may be, and probably is, that those races are incapable of assimilating the true meaning of sportsmanship as understood by the Anglo-Saxon . . .'

c 1550   *Terra Pacis* by Hendrik Niclaes published in Cologne mentions 'Kricket-staves'.

1766   Horace Walpole watched a game at Neuilly-sur-Seine, near Paris.

1768   Cricket at Spa, Austrian Netherlands.

1789   First tour to Paris aborted at Dover. French Revolution.

1793   Thomas Hope, a Dutch merchant of Amsterdam, portrayed by Sablet playing cricket in Rome.

1796   Description of cricket in German – in Hamburg publication *Games for the Young for the Recreation of Body and Spirit*.

1801   Danish translation by J Werfel of 1796 German book's cricket section. We read that 'the player A bowls the ball along the ground at speed to hit the rear wicket. Here the player B stands ready to grasp the ball and bowl it in the same manner at the front wicket. The ball is thus bowled continuously from one wicket to the other.' It is all in the eye of the beholder!

1810   Crawford's 'Light Division' played cricket at Lisbon.

1811   Club formed in Naples by Colonel Maceroni. Many French and Neapolitan officers as members.

1815   Match in June near Brussels watched by Duke of Wellington.

1829   Club in existence near Paris.

Other clubs were then established in **France**, i.e. Boulogne, Bordeaux, Calais, Dieppe, St Omer, St Servan, Arras, due extensively to the influx of lace-workers from Nottingham.

While the Emperor of France, Napoleon III, Empress and Prince Imperial were watching a game between Bickley Park and Beckenham, long-on held an extremely difficult catch. Shortly afterwards, a gentleman-in-waiting, hat doffed, went up to the elated fielder with a message from the Emperor which thanked him profusely for his spectacular performance and asked him to do it again.

Brussels CC became 'une societé royale' in 1977, an honour bestowed by HM King Baudouin. Five years before, the Rt Hon. Edward Heath, then British Prime Minister, became the first honorary patron.

OUT, TOVARICH

The Russians are credited with a desire to play cricket

'I am in mourning for my life – my charmed life that was thrice given back to me by the bourgeois-imperialist-capitalist-assassin fielding in the slips for the Wall Street-dominated profiteers and warmongers who are now known as MCC comrades.'

'But you are out, comrade. The little father of the white coat raised his finger.'

'True, comrade. And I am in mourning for my life because my runs-tally falls below the norm demanded by the Marxist-Leninist conception of opening-batsmen comrades of the Stakhanov class.'

'Batsmen-comrades who under-produce their norm may be shot. All the Selector-Commissars shall certainly be shot. As for you, comrade . . .'

'I go to the state shop to buy corpse candles for the Selector-Commissars. As for me, I must prepare for an invitation to a fraternal discussion with the inner-cell of the Supreme Soviet Cricket Co-operative. It will, I fear, be adieu.'

'The way ahead is dark, comrade. But perchance it shall be revealed.'

'The wicket had softened, comrade. Perchance the wicket had been watered by night by an agent of the unscrupulous British intelligence secretly introduced among the grounds-men-comrades of the motherland.'

'The nights are long, comrade. They are also cold. Let us buy corpse candles.'

'But the wicket, comrade. The little fathers of the Kremlin must be warned of the sabotage by the collective grounds-men. I shall, of course, confess my failure, but I shall declare in mitigation that the wicket was soft . . . the previous wicket was soft . . . all the wickets are soft . . . the next wickets . . .'

'They will be hard enough in Siberia, comrade.'

French comprehension: Monsieur Alphonse de Perpignan says, 'You English speak of your cricket in so funny ways and for a long time I do not understand him. But I have him now. At the Oval last week the wicket was what you call difficult, and when a ball from Carter hit him, four of him were down for 137 and the last of him had put on 58 runs. Is it not so?'

1855 Cricket club formed by university students at Utrecht in the **Netherlands**. Eighteen clubs in the 1880s and by 1891 two competitive leagues. The following year The Gentlemen of Holland toured England. Holland is now one of the two most powerful cricketing nations on the Continental mainland.

1860s Officially recorded matches in **Denmark** date from this period. There were games between Copenhagen and Sorø Academy teams. The Morild family made enormous contributions to the welfare of the game through several generations. Denmark ranks alongside Holland at the top of the Continental cricketing ladder.

Apparently, a Danish cricketer was so irate at being given out lbw first ball that he refused to stay for the rest of the match. Still fuming, he drove the seventy miles home from Copenhagen to Kalundborg. It was only later when the game was over that his team-mates discovered he had taken the coach in which they had travelled to the game that morning.

In **Germany** there have been clubs at Berlin, Karlsrühe, Frankfurt, Cologne and other cities and towns. The now famous Nuremberg cricketing publicity stamp, uncovered by Wendy and Marcus Williams, shows a local awareness in the early years of this century. In January 1985, Berlin's 'Cricket-Obmann', Kurt Rietz, turned 80.

According to the BBC radio commentator Brian Johnston, certain rumour had it that when Dartford became the first English club to visit Germany in 1931, the German umpires refused to call 'no ball' as it reflected on the manliness of their Aryan players.

A Lay and Wheeler Challenge match at Château de Thoiry, France, in the grounds of the Vicomtesse de la Panouse, between Essex and France in June 1991 saw Graham Gooch score 34 before being caught off the bowling of Sultan Shakzada. Neil Foster came in later to hit 61 off 55 balls. Essex (181) beat France (111) by 70 runs.

Switzerland has had cricket at Geneva, Zuoz College, in the Engadine Valley, and, if writer Andrew Lang is to be believed, in the market-place of Zug, where with a campstool for a wicket, the confrontation 'came to a sudden termination owing to a tremendous slog over the bowler's head going through the Burgomaster's window'.

In **Italy** in recent years a cricket association has been formed and a few years ago a joyously uninhibited band of Mediterranean cricketers came to the UK for a tour.

In **Portugal**, with clubs at Oporto and Lisbon, there have been visits from sides including those of T Westray and Sir Henry Leveson-Gower. Enthusiasm for the game sometimes waned, as can be seen from a letter to a club manager:

'Rua do Crucifixo, 7
Lisbon. 26th May 1875
My dear Jim,
I feel too seedy to play tomorrow for I have the shakes, and I calculate the sun would do me harm so please strike my name off the list.

Yours very truly,
JJ Ellerton.'

Again, an epistle from EV Wyse, of the Carcavelos Club, surmising that Lisbon CC were likely to lose the use of the ground at Campo Pequeno (impending construction of Bull Ring), also mentioned that his club was 'in a state of moult'.

A cutting from a Lisbon journal illustrates an amusing Portuguese view of the noble game:
'*Cricket Match*. Tomorrow there was to have come off an interesting game of cricket between the cricket clubs of Lisbon and Oporto. The object of the formation of these societies is the playing of the game of cricket-match, an active, running, driving, jumping game, which only can be played by a person having a good pair of legs, and in a climate where warm punch is found insufficient to keep up the animal heat. Does the reader know how to play a game at cricket-match? Two posts are placed at a great distance from one another. The player close to one of the posts throws a large ball towards the other party, who awaits the ball to send it far with a small stick with which he is armed. The other players then run to look after the ball, and while this search is going on the party who struck it with the stick runs incessantly from post to post, marking one for each run. It is plain, then, that it is to the advantage of the party who strikes the ball to make it jump very far. Sometimes it tumbles

into a thicket, and the players take hours before they can get hold of it, and all this time the player does not cease running from post to post, and marking points. Then those who find the ball arrive, exhausted, at the field of battle, and the one who has been running falls down half dead. At other times the projectile, sent with a vigorous arm, cannot be stopped and breaks the legs of the party who awaits it. The arrangements for the cricket-match include a sumptuous dinner in the marquee for fifty persons – an indispensable accompaniment to every cricket-match. We may, perhaps, assist at this great battle, and hope the committee will place us at a safe distance from the combatants, where the principles of the game can be seen with the help of an opera glass.'

'Watching Graeme Hick yesterday – not at his most iridescent but still over-qualified for the game everyone else was playing – recalled the story about an attendant at Florence's Uffizi Gallery. "Remember, signor," he told an American tourist, "here it is not the paintings that are on trial."'

Michael Henderson,
Worcestershire v Yorkshire,
The Guardian

When an MCC side visited **Paris** in 1867 under the captaincy of RA Fitzgerald, the local reaction underlined historian GM Trevelyan's general premise that the heads of the French *noblesse* might not have rolled so speedily some seven decades earlier if they had been capable of playing cricket with their peasants.

A resident remarked to Fitzgerald: 'It's a truly magnificent game, but I cannot understand why you do not engage a

'Garçon!'
French nobleman
has a job for a
'lower order' player

servant to field for you instead of having so much running about to do yourself.'

Cricket in **Latvia** started and stopped with surprising suddenness. A club was started in the capital, Riga, and during their first game a policeman, who had been sent to observe and report, decided he could find out more by standing among the infielders.

His conscientiousness proved counter-productive. Having refused to heed well-meant warnings regarding his safety from the players, he soon stopped a ball with his head. Proof surely for any Baltic bureaucrat that this foreign pastime was both undesirable and highly dangerous. The municipality forbade cricket forthwith.

> *A* Daily Telegraph *editorial speculated that with bilingualism à la mode at Radley College, it would not be too long before one of their First XI bowlers got the other team's captain* jambe *before* guichet. *'They should not be surprised if their concerted yell of "*Comment cela?*" gets short shrift from the umpire.'*

Russia: Before the 1917 Revolution the land of the Czars contained two clubs for certain, possibly more, the St Petersburg and the Alexandrossky, but the grounds were so rough and uneven that extras usually exceeded individual scores. Apparently, Nicholas II liked the game and actually had a cricket pitch prepared in the grounds of the Imperial Palace at Peterhof. Perhaps his interest sprang from being told of the occasion when Nicholas I attended a match on Chatham Lines and having watched for a few minutes remarked: 'I don't wonder at the courage of you English when you teach your children to play with cannon balls.' Not long ago, in a bookshop in Helsinki, a booklet of some fifty pages with a dozen illustrations was discovered. It contained a concise history of cricket and an account of its laws. Simply entitled *Cricket, the English Ball Game*, the work was written by M Volkov in the pre-revolutionary alphabet and published by MO Volf of Petrograd and Moscow in 1915, not exactly the most propitious time to maximise sales.

Maybe the book was not unconnected to the group of students at St Petersburg, one of whom translated the laws into Russian. As he had no English acquaintance to check his interpretation, according to him the wickets were placed only twelve feet apart and no fieldsman was allowed within forty feet of the batsmen – added to which, the non-striker's role in running between wickets was totally ignored.

The consequence was that the striker set up some kind of record, simply by jumping to the opposite crease and back again. He not only scored a hundred in ten minutes and put his non-striking partner in constant peril with blows all over the body, he also intimidated the bowler.

Lapland. Home-made bats and balls were used in a six-a-side, single-wicket game by the inhabitants of the Kola Peninsula. 'The match was attended from beginning to end with shouts of *Horosho! Horosho igrali!* (Good! Well played!) and loud laughter . . . Thus was *Angelo-kaya igra* introduced into Russian Lapland.' Keenness was such that one match ended late at night and another started at one o'clock in the morning.

Finland. During the 1980s an enterprising band of cricket-lovers produced *The Helsinki Cricketer* magazine.

The Malaga Cricket Association has been running the Costa del

'OUR CONSTITUTION IS THE POST TRUE BATSMEN WILL DEFEND'

by Christopher Kemp

The cricketing cracks of the year '89
Felt a sociable tour of fair France would be fine;
But no English bowler delivered an over,
Since his Grace turned them back when he met them at Dover.

What gallant, what elegant, games might have been
In front of the château where, perched by the green,
The Count and the Countess would welcome the sport
Far from the cliques and corruptions of court!

Who knows? The curé might have stopped at the spot
And stood at square leg to say whether, or not,
Some rustical swiper was stumped or run out
When 'Comment est celà?' was the questioning shout.

In the sweet shades of the flower-bedecked tent
The thirsty contestants from Yorkshire and Kent
Would not have disdained the cool cup of Vouvray
Or Entre-deux-mers, brought round in a tray.

Such stylish French hundreds, immaculate knocks,
Applauded, perhaps, by the brown Charles James Fox,
Across for the cricket, the chat and the fizz
And suave strolls by the Loire with his own dearest Liz.

Our breakfasting gentry, taking their toast
With steaming French coffee, *The Times* and the *Post*,
Might have checked on the rumour which proved to be true
That Provence were 600 for 3, v. Anjou.

But as our trim cricketers roved to the pub
The Frenchmen turned in to their Jacobin club,
Where they picked up their Rights, put their cricket bags down
And paraded in tricolour all round the town.

Danton, the demon, then summoned his strength,
(Wide, wild and furious; no hint of good length)
With a hop, skip and jump he hurled into the ring
The guillotined head of the last capet king.

'This is simply too much' thought Prime Minister Pitt,
'Our line is cricket, and claret, and wit',
While Porissot and Pouzot in Anglophobe oaths
Bawled at Britannia to fit some new clothes.

Before they had given the form a good look
They started a Test, which was not in the book,
In a game for *La Gloire*, a French pastime, in which
Twenty-two miles is the length of the pitch.

King George was delighted, and every French jerk
Had already been no-balled by vigilant Burke,
SO JACK AND HORATIO STOOD TO THEIR WICKET
TO PROVE THAT EQUALITY JUST WASN'T CRICKET.

Sol cricket festival for several years which has attracted attention to the game in **Spain**. A number of English professionals have been there helping with tuition, including Pat Pocock, ex-Surrey and England. In the last twelve years of the nineteenth century, Marquis de Santa Susana, Anthony Benitez de Lugo, President of Surrey, produced two books about the club and one on its champion batsman, Walter Read. The books were for private circulation and published by the firm of Ricardo Fé in Madrid. In 1989, the Madrid CC issued its first annual with all the contents in both English and Spanish.

POLITICAL CRICKET

Cricketing Parliamentarians can be identified very easily. Whenever the interval bell rings to herald the return of the umpires in a Test or county game, they are the ones who spring to their feet immediately, wearing among other things an anxious look. Just for a moment they are back in the House with a Whip to hand and a vote to cast . . .

'Most would agree that Parliament must continue to exist. While it does so, the two parties must play a game modelled, apparently, on that of cricket: a game in which no innings can be prolonged for ever.'

C Northcote Parkinson,
The Law of Delay

Sir William Gage of Firle, MP for Seaford, was one of the earliest patrons of cricket. Early in the eighteenth century he mounted several matches with the Duke of Richmond at Goodwood.

Lord Tankerville, Postmaster General when William Pitt was Prime Minister, was, according to a newspaper of the time, 'renowned for nothing but cricket playing, bruising, and keeping of low company'.

On 29 August 1796, 'Mr Thos. Paine – Authour of the rights of Man' was present at a meeting of the Hambledon Club. At that time, Citizen Tom Paine, who had taken up residence in Paris, was under sentence of death *in absentia* on a charge of treason. Nobody knows why he attended the meeting.

Playing cricket with Mr Babington, a ball struck my foot with great violence and by the positive injunctions of my surgeon, I have ever since been sentenced to a sofa.

William Wilberforce, 1810

The Attorney-General, speaking in the House of Commons in August 1843, said that it was perfectly legal for persons to play cricket on Sundays after Divine Service, if the play took place within their own parish; but if they went out of their parish they were punishable.

Lord Charles Russell was Sergeant-at-Arms of the House of Commons for 27 years, author of several booklets on cricket as well as a number of articles, member of MCC for 67 years and President in 1835, participant in 'Tom Brown's Match' against Rugby in 1841 and subject of a doggerel song written and performed by Benjamin Aislabie, secretary of MCC. One couplet runs:

What is all this noise about? And
why this wondrous bustle?
All the world comes out to see
my noble Lord Charles Russell.

Aidan Crawley, Oxford University, Kent and Buckinghamshire – highest score 204 for the Varsity v Northants – had a notable career as a journalist and author and was at one time editor-in-chief of ITN. He was Labour MP for Buckingham 1945–51, before crossing the House a decade later when he represented West Derbyshire from 1962–7 as a Conservative.

A Parliamentary duo of then current and ex-Sports Ministers, Robert Atkins and Colin Moynihan, managed a stand of 48 for a team led by the last Shah of Iran's one-time financial ad-viser, Bertie Joel. The opposition were the Lord's Taverners. In fact, at the time of the encounter, Moynihan was Junior Energy Minister and obviously found enough to spare to score 48 not out off his own bat.

Crossing the floor of the House – or just practising his running between the wickets?

Charles Stewart Parnell was active in the cricket fraternity of County Carlow during the middle of the last century and was later a member of the well-known Na Shuler Club.

> Revd John Mitford eulogising the great Silver Billy Beldham: 'His peculiar glory was the cut. Here he stood with no man beside him, the laurel was all his own, it was like the cut of a racket. His wrist seemed to turn on springs of the finest steel. He took the ball as Burke did the House of Commons, between wind and water; not a moment too soon or late.'

> 'I used to enjoy cricket, except for one game during the holidays when we were playing up against a telegraph pole. I was the stumper and when I turned suddenly to stop a ball, I hit that pole and broke one of my front teeth clean in two. It was with me for ages because there wasn't any question of going to the dentist. You had to pay for the dentist and we didn't have any money.'
>
> Joe Gormley, former NUM President, *Battered Cherub*

Lamplugh Freckville Ballantine-Dykes, who once made 58 for a Public Schools XI v 'The World' at Bengal, was a driving force behind the formation of a Cumberland CCC in the 1880s. As John Hurst reveals in his book on the County Club, a reply to Dyke's letter seeking support came from Sir Wilfred Lawson, Liberal MP for Carlisle and Cockermouth, who became a Vice-President:

> *Dear Lamplugh, I'm willing to join*
> *Your club in the orthodox way,*
> *But first have the goodness to state*
> *Who is it you wish me to play?*

> *I'm awfully fond of the game;*
> *In fact, there's nothing like cricket.*
> *So if Musgrave's the party you name*
> *I'll at once undertake single wicket.*

> *I'll bowl at his legs, for that place*
> *Would stand me, I think, in good stead.*
> *For when fighting with that sort of man*
> *There's no use if you bowl at his head*

> *And so to the contest of cricket*
> *I'll manage my poem to drop,*
> *For Johnny I'll get a keep wicket*
> *And David shall be my long-stop.*

(Musgrave was almost certainly a political opponent and David was likely to be David Ainsworth, Liberal MP for Cumberland in 1880.)

Dykes died after long ill-health caused, it was said, by an injury sustained at cricket. Sir Wilfred Lawson's son, Sir Wilfred of Isel, another MP and cricket lover, kept wicket when in his seventies. In a match against Maryport Church Guild, a fast rising ball hit him in the mouth, breaking two teeth and lacerating his face. 'Undaunted, he visited the dentist – who pulled a third tooth – returned to the cricket ground and would have won the match for Isel had he not been run out in trying to make a sixth run off a hit!' Lawson passed away on the cricket field, dying almost instantaneously after collapsing while batting.

In November 1922 Pat Purcell, then a young man in the Irish Republican Army, and a few of his colleagues dragged the son of the founder of Carlow Cricket Club, Horace Rochfort, from his carriage on his way from the clubhouse. On a freezing cold night, they tied Rochfort with rope and towed him up and down the River Barrow for some time before returning him to the seat of his carriage.

The action was part of the reprisals against a policy of terror used by some Carlow landlords. The next Rochfort put his estate for sale and further threats and intimidation saw the disintegration of the cricket club at that time.

Rochfort senior, a member of the leisured class, was a slow under-arm bowler who used to start his run-up about ten yards from the wicket and then would stop every few steps and put the ball to his eye until he bowled the ball. There is a story that in a match between Phoenix and Carlow – two of the premier sides in Ireland – 'there was a young Lieutenant Ricardo batting for Phoenix who, when Rochfort (playing for Carlow) began to advance, would walk about his wicket and be back just in time to play the ball'.

Cricket provided active entertainment for some of the participants at the 1991 Commonwealth Conference in Harare, Zimbabwe. Prime Ministers Bob Hawke of Australia and John Major of Great Britain faced the first four overs of a charity game, to be replaced at the crease by President Gayoom of The Maldives and PM Nawaz Sharif of Pakistan, who hit three sixes in an innings of 31 from 15 balls. The next pairing were the Pakistan Foreign Secretary, Shaharyar Khan, and Prime Minister Kennedy Simmonds of St Kitts-Nevis. The bowling came from Commonwealth Secretary-General Chief Emeka Anyaoku of Nigeria and Uganda's High Commissioner to London, George Kirya. Grenada's PM, Nicholas Braithwaite, umpired.

Lord Monckton was a member of Churchill's Cabinet and the MCC. He remarked that 'in comparison, the Cabinet seemed like a bunch of communists'.

The notorious fraudster, Horatio Bottomley, one-time Liberal MP for South Hackney, Club President and occasional player for Dicker, was well liked even when in prison. He paid for the club's first pavilion.

A Conservative peeress thought Les Ames was a French restaurant.

'I have batted on all sorts of wickets. I have stood up to all kinds of bowling, bodyline bowling included – to say nothing of barracking. And having presided over a Tory

Cabinet, I have witnessed every manifestation of human nature. And having done that I am now prepared to face the Committee of the MCC.'

Earl Baldwin of Bewdley on his appointment as President of MCC

A civil servant, whose official tasks involved drafting replies to Parliamentary questions in the House, was driving with a passenger en route to a cricket tour in Cornwall when he lost his way. He stopped and asked of a native 'Where am I?' To which came the reply: 'You be in your car.' Turning to his companion, the civil servant said: 'That is a perfect example of an ideal reply to a Parliamentary question. It is brief, factual and relevant but contributes precisely nothing to the subject.'

Once again he looked at the yokel – who actually was not, but that is how he thought of him – and at the same time pointed to his cricket bat on the back seat. 'What be that?' asked the short-sighted countryman. 'A piece of wood!' came the snappy response from the civil servant.

PM John Major, no mean cricketer, has expressed interest in the idea of a match between a Prime Minister's XI and the touring side, as long as he can pick the team.

Lord Hawke (nephew of the great Yorkshireman) had bowled his tempting 'slows' for two overs and a lot of runs. The first four balls of his third over were hit for two, six, four, six, at which point came a declaration. Hawke frowned and then was heard to mutter: 'Pity, just when I'd got him guessing!'

In a game between Lords and Commons and MCC, a batsman for the Headquarters Club was given out caught at the wicket just as the tea interval was due. During the break he complained bitterly about the dismissal, claiming that his bat had been nowhere near the ball. So much so, that he was invited to return to the crease by the Parliamentarians' captain, Sir Charles Mott-Radclyffe. As the batsman prepared to face the remaining balls of the pre-interval over, the umpire, Denis Howell, MP, said: 'Who's that? I gave him out before tea.' 'Oh, he said he wasn't out and so the captain said he could come back,' explained the nearest fielder. 'Oh, did he?' said Howell. 'Well, that's the last time I shall umpire for this team.'

Wing Commander Sir Eric Bullus, MP for Wembley North, wrote a book on his memories of Lords and Commons cricket over a quarter of a century. He recalls Aidan Crawley's hat-trick against Fares Sarofeem's XI, an Egyptian touring side, at the Oval in 1951. All three batsmen were lbw. In the same match Lord Dunglass (now Lord Home of the Hirsel) opened the batting and scored 24. He also took 1 for 4 in the only two balls he bowled. Lords and Commons won by 4 wickets.

Edward Cakobau, one-time Deputy Prime Minister of Fiji, turned out for several London clubs after World War Two.

Cakobau, a Fijian and a half-brother to Queen Salote of Tonga, was a scintillating cricketer – a brilliant all-rounder who always played in bare feet and wore the traditional Fijian white skirt.

'I was obsessed by the game. It occupied most of my adolescence. I was just good enough at cricket to play morning as well as afternoon, and winter as well as summer, but not good enough to get into the 1st XI. I used to enjoy myself in the field repeating all the poetry I knew, which took a long time.'

Sir Keith Joseph, interviewed by Terry Coleman

'It is paradoxical the way the opposition to the Government is coming from the most unexpected quarters. But then I like that sort of thing. I'm the sort of person who likes to play cricket in northern Greenland.'

Lord Shackleton on the Lords, 30 April 1988

Home Secretary in 1922, First Lord of the Admiralty in 1924, MP for Oswestry for 23 years, William Clive Bridgeman was a middle-order right-hand batsman who had gained a cricket blue at Cambridge and then played for Shropshire, Staffordshire and MCC. He was created a Viscount in 1929.

The Rt Hon Sir Winston S Churchill, KG, OM, CH, MP, armed with large brandy and larger cigar and in conversation

'I once saw a bowler in Australia thunder to the wicket and bowl a flat-out under-arm to the batsman. No warning given. Quite rightly too. In my profession you have to mystify the enemy.'
Field-Marshal Viscount Montgomery

with Max Aitken and Ian Peebles, described a chequered cricketing career which terminated at the age of ten with a broken finger. There was some difficulty in recalling the terms and implements and also in pronouncing the letter S:

'The ball came pasht and hit the little thingsh behind – eh – schtumps – yes.'

The Hon. Thomas De Grey, who became the sixth Baron Walsingham, would have gained three cricket blues for Cambridge University but for an unfortunate attack of rheumatism. Reckoned at one time the best shot in the country, he bagged a record 1070 grouse in a single day. MP for West Norfolk, 1865–70.

'Any cricketer would want to bowl to Bradman even if he were to hit them for six. It's the same with Robin,' said Brian Walden, former MP and now TV interviewer, referring to politicians queuing to be lashed by Robin Day's tongue.

After an inter-county match, in which Sussex defeated Kent at Lewes in 1735, John Whaley wrote to his pupil Horace

Walpole commenting that 'they seem as much pleased as if they had got an election. We have been at supper with them all and have left them at this one o'clock in the morning laying betts about the next match.'

'The atmosphere reminded me of a minor public school. On the face of it, life was a mixture of the

> 'If we all had our friends checked at cricket matches we'd have no friends and no cricket.'
> John Le Carré, A Perfect Spy

quaint and the archaic. Every year the Office virtually closed to attend the Lord's Test Match where MI5 had an unofficial patch in the Lord's Tavern.'
Peter Wright, Spycatcher

Peter Wright: 'MI5 had an unofficial patch in the Lord's Tavern'

Matthew Engel, commenting in *The Guardian* on John Major's knowledge of cricket statistics, wondered about economic planning. 'The estimate for next year's government spending of £201 billion, for instance, bears a suspicious resemblance to Alf Gover's total of first-class wickets in 1937.'

CRICKET IN COURT

The legal eagles have snared
many an unfortunate cricketer.
There follows an arbitrary
selection of some of these who
have found themselves in a little
difficulty with the law. Many of
the inclusions owe much to John
Scott's exhaustive study, *Caught
in Court*.

John Shilton, Warwickshire
cricketer, in jail in Capetown for
theft by false pretences, was on
one occasion smuggled out to
play for the warders' team
against that of the De Beers
mining company.

A narrow escape for De Beers

In Denis Compton's first match for Middlesex, batting at number eleven, umpire William Bestwick gave him out lbw. Bestwick, who years earlier had been involved in an intemperate fracas which resulted in a coroner's jury returning a verdict of justifiable homicide, had a liking for drink. 'Gubby' Allen, who had been partnering Compton, remarked to Bestwick: 'Bill, that wasn't a very good decision, was it?', to which Bestwick replied: 'Very sorry, Mr Allen, I had to pump ship.'

In 1943, Learie Constantine won a case against the Imperial Hotel, Russell Square, London, for breach of its 'common law duty as an innkeeper' after they had reneged on a confirmed room booking. The basis of the charge was racial discrimination.

In 1855, during a game at Templecombe in Somerset, a man named Tucker was killed by

Out – cross-legged before wicket . . .

being crushed between shunted railway trucks while he was looking for the ball which had been hit on to the line.

David Colson, a teacher of Rushmoor School in Bedford, who was sacked for striking the bottoms of his pupils with a cricket bat, was, according to the decision of an Industrial Tribunal, unfairly dismissed.

On Easter Day, 1611, 'Bartholomew Wyatt and Richard Latter, two young parishioners of Sidlesham, near Chichester, played cricket instead of attending worship at their parish church'.

For their sins, the youths were required to appear before a court held in Chichester Cathedral where they were fined one shilling and made to do penance.

NOTICE!
Take notice all, That from this thicket
You may cut stumps for your cricket,
But never let me catch you at
Cutting down a tree for a bat

Posted on the paling of a magistrate's property at Goudhurst, Kent, in 1860.

'The interview actually means getting a guy out of a cell for five minutes, talking about cricket, putting him back into the cell and turning it into a forty-five-minute confession.'
Metropolitan Police Constable interviewed by Roger Graf in *Talking Blues*

Arthur Coningham, who played one Test for Australia and took a wicket with his first ball, tried to divorce his wife for adultery with a priest. In court, Mrs Coningham related how she and O'Haran, the priest, met 'to indulge' every Friday, because Saturday was his weekly visit to confession. Coningham failed to get his divorce, although eleven years later, in 1912, Mrs Coningham managed to divorce *him* for committing adultery in a beach hut. It was all too much for Coningham. 'In Sydney,' he told a reporter, 'my wife said she did and a jury said she didn't. In Wellington [in the interim the Coninghams had emigrated to New Zealand] I said I didn't and a jury said I did.'

Nicholas Hunt sued William Wood after he had failed to deliver the twelve candles won in a wager on a cricket match at Coxheath in 1646.

William Waterfall was charged at a coroner's inquest with unlaw-fully killing George Twigg in a cricket match on Bakewell Common in 1775. Waterfall was found guilty of manslaughter and imprisoned for nine months. He was also punished by having his left hand burnt.

George Rimington, a barrister-at-law, keeping wicket in a match at a lunatic asylum, was warned by one of the inmates who was batting: 'Don't stump me. I am Nebuchadnezzar and I can strike you dead.'

The colourful turban worn by Kumar Sri Ranjitsinhji has been wrapped in a legal dispute over ownership. For twenty years the red and gold turban was in the trophy cabinet at Ilkley Cricket Club. In 1991, the club decided to auction the 21-foot headcloth to help raise funds to buy its ground from Bradford Council, but the sale was postponed because the son of former Ilkley captain Jack Brumfitt – who was given it at second or third hand – claims it is still family property.

In 1984, Dennis Lillee was suspended by the Australian Cricket Board after an altercation with the umpires in a Sheffield Shield match over drinks on the field of play. Lillee served a court order and the case was heard in the Supreme Court of Western Australia which ruled that the ban be upheld.

Vallance Jupp, Sussex and Northants all-rounder in a career lasting thirty years, was impris-oned for manslaughter after a road accident in which there were several injuries and a death.

In 1978, Bedford Industrial Tribunal dismissed West Indian Test bowler Bishen Bedi's claim against Northamptonshire CCC for unfair dismissal. Counsel for the club, Stuart McKinnion (himself no mean performer with bat and ball for Purley) con-tended that Bedi was employed only for the cricket season. 'After all,' said McKinnion, 'Father Christmas cannot be regarded as employed throughout the year.'

Frank Foster, Warwickshire captain and England Test all-rounder, who had a glittering career before the First World War, was found guilty of obtaining money by false pretences and credit by fraud in 1950. He was put on probation for a year.

In 1974, Malcolm Green's six-year-old son had his skull fractured by a cricket ball struck from a game at the village ground in Little Waltham, Essex. Green took revenge by setting fire to the pavilion causing over £1000 worth of damage. He pleaded guilty to arson and received a suspended sentence.

Complaining about the lack of Test Match coverage from Australia, Judge Michael Argyle at the Old Bailey commented: 'It's enough to make an Orthodox Jew want to join the Nazi Party.'

Judge James Pickles has been described as the 'Geoffrey Boycott of the Bench'.

Leslie Hylton, the West Indian fast bowler, shot his wife. Miles Giffard, the Cornish batsman, killed his parents and Arie Molenaar, a leading Dutch cricketer, helped murder a shopkeeper.

WHAT'S IN A NAME?

If we believe Marshall McLuhan when he says that 'the name of a man is a numbing blow from which he never recovers', there are a few that follow who were in deep trouble . . .

From 1805 to 1837, twelve major matches were played by the famous B Eleven against the best in England. Cricketers whose surnames began with the second letter of the alphabet were eligible. Their standard can be gauged from such celebrated individuals as Beauclerk, Budd, Beldham, Beagley and Broadbridge.

In 1867, eleven of Lord Lyttelton's family defeated Bromsgrove Grammar School by 10 wickets.

Keeping up with the Joneses has been a continual chore for members of the Boughton Hall XI (Chester) and Tattenhall CC. For practically a hundred years from the 1890s, it has been rare to find either one or the other of the sides without the cricketing prowess of a Jones reflected on the scorecard – from Mr William Jones to his sons WE, LN and HR to his grandsons WHR, EL, BE, BS; and the list is not complete.

William Jones, captain of Tattenhall and a magistrate to boot, took all 10 wickets for 17 runs against Bunbury in 1899. Extraordinarily, his sons WE and LN, both of whom also played for Cheshire, emulated his feat. LN took 10 for 2 playing for Tattenhall against Whitechurch in 1909 and WE, turning out for Boughton Hall against Huyton in 1926, took 10 for 43. Possibly, a unique treble.

Six members of the Mann family played for Cogenhoe CC in Northamptonshire at the beginning of this century. It was perhaps not surprising as the marriages of five brothers produced 20 children and one of the brothers had 15 grandchildren. Tim Street quoted a saying in his centenary history which read: 'If one met a woman in Cogenhoe she was probably a Mann!'

On 2 January 1992, the names of four Pringles were to be found on cricket scorecards. In New Zealand, Auckland and England were contesting a one-day affair in which DR (England), C and MR were involved. And in Capetown, South Africa, MW was obtaining 5 for 57 for Western Province against Transvaal.

The appropriately-named five Quinns – Paddy, Frank, Gerry, Kevin and Brendon (the first four brothers) – all learnt their cricket at Belvedere College and during the 1930s often played together for the oldest existing club in Ireland, Phoenix.

CLASSIC PLAYERS

LW Jenkinson in the Cricket Society's splendid *Journal* surmised how a team drawn from classical antiquity might look:

1. Grace, WG .... Gloucestershire
2. Bacchus, SFA .... West Indies
3. Homer, HWF .... Minor Counties
4. Grace, EM .... Gloucestershire
5. Caesar, Julius .... Surrey
6. Constantine, LN .... West Indies
7. Felix, N .... Kent/Surrey
8. Paris, CGA .... Hampshire
9. Grace, GF .... Gloucestershire
10. Alexander, FCM .... West Indies
11. Hector, PA .... Essex

Mr Jenkinson added that he was tempted to include Castor, BK, in a misguided attempt to persuade himself that the natural pairing would be with Pollux (Graeme and Peter)! Perhaps one should be 12th man and the others extra substitutes for inevitable injuries.

Charles Absolon was a remarkable and well-liked all-round cricketer who experienced phenomenal success in club cricket, largely in the London area. It is impossible to estimate accurately the vast number of runs and wickets that Absolon captured in his long career. Always much in demand, he continued playing to a high standard in old age. He scored 1029 runs and took 103 wickets in his seventy-second year and at the age of seventy-eight he twice performed the hat-trick.

Charles Absolom was a notable all-round athlete – at Cambridge he represented the university at putting the shot and the long jump, as well as gaining a blue at cricket. He was also a good footballer. He played for Kent and Essex and was selected for one Test against Australia, being regarded as an attacking batsman with unorthodox shots and a medium pace bowler. He toured America in the last decade of his life, associating himself with the causes of the 'Red Indians', and died in excruciating pain when, employed as a purser on a ship loading sugar-cane in Port of Spain, Trinidad, he was crushed by a falling crane. He took three days to die.

In 1926, *The Cricketer* ran a competition on novel lines asking readers to add names, dates and sides to lists in various categories. The surnames were of players who had taken part in 'matches of note', i.e. first-class; others contested by the county and minor county sides; the Gentlemen of ——; well-known clubs, colleges or schools; and good scratch sides. Some of these names are reproduced here, together with a few more:

NATURAL HISTORY
Almond, Raison, Beet, Root.
Birds: Bird, Buzzard, Capon, Cockerell, Crane, Duck, Finch, Gull, Hawke, Martin, Nightingale, Partridge, Peacock, Raven, Robins, Rook, Sheldrake, Sparrow, Starling, Swallow, Swan, Swift, Teale, Woodcock.
Beasts: Badger, Bear, Buck, Bugg, Bull, Bullock, Fox, Hind, Hogg, Hunter, Leech, Lyon, Mare, Mole, Roe, Roebuck, Steer.
Fishes: Dolphin, Fish, Herring, Otter, Pike, Salmon, Whale.

When Peter Willey faced fast bowler Michael Holding in a Test Match encounter between England and the West Indies, the commentator remarked: 'The bowler's Holding, the batsman's Willey.'

Trees, Shrubs, etc: Ash, Beech, Birch, Elms, Oakes, Bean, Berry, Brann, Budd, Burr, Cherry, Cobb, Flowers, Hay, Heather, Hedges, Lavender, Leaf, Leman, Lilley, Mace, Moss, Mustard, Nettle, Nutt, Orange, Peach, Peel, Pepper, Plant, Plum (nickname), Rice, Root, Rose, Roseblade, Rye, Salt, Stocks, Thorne, Twigg, Vine.
Places: Brooks, Bush, Cliff, Common, Craig, Dale, Down, Dyke, Field, Forrest, Glen, Heath, Hill, Lake, Lane, Mead, Moor, Orchard, Pool, Quarry, Rhodes, Street, Vale, Waterfall, Weir, Wells, Woods.
Various: Brown, Breeze, Clay, Cutbush, Dew, Frost, Gale, Mold, Nest, Weeding.

THE CHURCH
Beadle, Clark(e), Sexton.
Abbot, Allchurch, Bishop, Christian, Church, Creed,

THE KNIGHTS OF CRICKET

Sir Francis Lacey

Sir Pelham 'Plum' Warner

Sir Henry Leveson-Gower

Sir Frederick Toone

Sir Jack Hobbs

Sir Vijay Anand, The
   Rajkumar of Vizianagram

Sir Donald Bradman

Sir Leonard Hutton

Sir Learie Constantine

Sir Frank Worrell

Sir Neville Cardus

Sir Garfield Sobers

Sir George 'Gubby' Allen

Sir Richard Hadlee

Sir Colin Cowdrey

Crozier, Deacon, Dean, Fryer, Heaven, Kirk, Monk, Nunn, Parsons, Pope, Priestley, Prior, Sanctuary.

TRADES, OCCUPATIONS AND PROFESSIONS
Baker, Barber, Brazier, Brewer, Butcher, Butler, Carpenter, Carter, Carver, Chancellor, Chandler, Collier, Constable, Cook, Cooper, Diver, Docker, Draper, Driver, Dyer, Farmer, Fisher, Forester, Fowler, Gardiner, Goldsmith, Groom, Hawker, Hewer, Hopper, Huntsman, Mason, Miller, Nutter, Ostler, Page, Painter, Piper, Plummer, Potter, Proctor, Rider, Sadler, Salter, Sellers, Seneschal, Sergeant, Shepherd, Shoesmith, Skinner, Skipper, Slater, Smith, Spicer, Stabler, Stoner, Tester, Thresher, Tinker, Tipper, Tyler, Usher, Warden, Washer, Weaver, Writer, Walker.

CRICKET TERMS
Bale, Ball, Bat (Gents v Players, 1827), Bayles, Bowler, Chance, Colt, Creese, Field, Fielder, Fielding, Fluke, Gamble, Greenfield, Grounds, Grubb, Knox, Kortright, Light, Luck, Meadows, Mead, Over, Park, Player, Punchard, Scorer.

VARIOUS
Abel and Cain; Adam, Eve and Eden; Abraham and Moses. Day and Martin and Shine (all played for Kent).
Anguish, Paine, Joy and Peace. Bigg, Little, Broad, Short, Large, Small, Low, Long.
Evill, Faithful, Gentle, Good, Jolly, Nice, Noble, Perfect, Pretty, Proud, Tidy, Toogood, Valiant, Vane, Wild, Wise.
Bagge, Box, Case.
East, North, West.
Penny, Tanner, Twopenny.
Child, Doll, Kidd, Mann, Naumann, Suckling, Talboys.
Blunt, Round, Sharp.
Boddy, Brain, Foot, Hands, Head, Hide, Knee, Legg, Blood and Bone.
Boot (& Boots), Buckle, Capes, Coates, Cuff, Diamond, Hankey, Hatt, Rubie, Studd, Tye.
Boyle and Fry.
Young and Old.
Single and Batchelor.
King, Knight, Lord, Duke, Earl, Prince, Squire.

Curious, associated and exotic names have included Bancalari, de Kerschendorf, Dracopoli, Hogsflesh, Tarbox, Marx, Sua, A'Court, Ablack, Bacmeister, Bastard, in fact, anybody and everybody from Adolph Christian Ernest Von Ernsthausen, Xenophon Balaskas, Lodovick Bligh and the Honourable Seton Robert de la Poer Horsley to Leonidas De Toledo Marcondes De Montezuma, who was born in Crowborough and died in Dartford. Artistic and moral licence might even allow a joining together of Bissex and Uel.

FS Ashley-Cooper, who was the brain behind the competition, employed two maids called Ball and Bowler. He recalled going downstairs early one morning and seeing them come out of the dining-room with a sweep. When asked what his name was, he replied: 'Over, sir.'

'HOW OUT' DECISIONS RECORDED IN SCOREBOOKS
Put out behind the Yold
(H Palmer playing for Coulsdon
v Chertsey, 1775)
Hit himself out
Shambled out
Nipt out
Gave out wrongfully
Gave out
Out below the elbow
Hit wicket after remembering what he had forgotten
Run out – who batted shamefully
Given out 'because the umpire could no longer bear to watch a

man in an MCC sweater batting so badly'
'Blockball – dead in dispute'
'Caught grey-haired gentleman at deep fine-leg'

An informative and amusing 'Cricketer's Diary' by Middlesex and Durham bowler Simon Hughes in *The Independent* produced a glossary of some modern cricketing terms:
Jaffa ball that pitches leg and hits off
Banana balls big swingers
Grenades bowler tossing it up
Darts spinner bowling flat
Throatball bouncer destined for the oesophagus
'Get it up in' bowler being encouraged to bowl throatball
Aerosol bowling someone spraying it everywhere, out of control
Cafeteria/buffet attack one on which batsmen can help themselves

Good counter, Casio batsman who always pinches a single shot off the last ball
German General (Goebbels) shot tickling towards boundary
Grabbers, snafflers slip fielders
Cardboard cut-outs captains who stand immobile at first slip
Donkey outfielder (usually more than 14 stones)
Dollies stumps
'The word flat-bat, formerly used to describe a flail on the off-side, now has official recognition from MCC. The double-faced blade developed by two bat companies may now be seen on the field, particularly in the hands of batsmen proficient in the reverse sweep.' Nevertheless, with no hump at the back of the bat and therefore no overdrive or 'sweet spot', an attempt to loft one over mid-off could see the ball 'lob gently back to the bowler. They will then be relabelled "planks".'

EVEN ODDS
AND ENDS

A deuced odd there and a loose end here! What's going on? Let us find out . . .

The York cricket club is one of the oldest in the country and had two recognised grounds. The better ground was on the Knavesmire, the racecourse home of the Gimcrack Stakes and Ebor Handicap; the other, Heworth Moor, where, according to the articles of association in 1784, members were bidden to assemble at 4 a.m. and were fined if not ready to play as the Minster clock chimed five.

'A Cricket Match between the Upper Mitcham Early-Rising Association versus Lower Mitcham Peep-O'-Day Club will be played on Lower Mitcham Green, on Wednesday mornings, July 6th and 13th, 1870. Wickets to be pitched at 3.30 a.m. Play to commence at 4 precisely. Stumps to be drawn at 7 o'clock each morning.' After which, some of the players set off to do a day's work in the surrounding lavender and herb fields.

John Bowyer, a printer cutter by trade, was an outstanding left-hand batsman for Surrey in the early part of the nineteenth century. He first played at Lord's in 1810 when he helped Surrey beat England by 8 wickets. More often he played at Mitcham, where he had been born in 1790.

Lord Nelson, who frequently watched cricket on the Green, gave a shilling to Bowyer prior to Trafalgar and told him: 'Drink confusion to the French.'

Sir Joseph Cotterill, who appeared in 27 matches for Sussex during the 1870s and 80s, had an enviable reputation for throwing the cricket ball. His best authenticated throw was 121 yards in 1875. He became an eminent surgeon.

Christmas Day cricket took place at Putney in 1888, when two sides were captained by GH Harnett and M Forrum of the Pall Mall Wanderers.

In the 1796 clash between one-legged Greenwich Pensioners and an eleven of one-armed players, there were five broken legs – all wooden. That did not stop the 'peggers' winning by 111 runs.

The Beddington Club decided to carry on playing cricket in 1940, despite the loss of many of their side to the Forces. Older, semi-retired members turned out in games against 'old boys' from other clubs. 'This went on until the end of August, when the Battle of Britain, often fought directly overhead, stopped games while the players sought shelter under trees.' Echoes of Wellington's claim that battles were won on the playing fields . . .

Cricket has been chanced on several occasions on the treacherous Goodwin Sands. One encounter took place on 10 August 1854 after Morris Thompson of Walmer had challenged Captain Pearson of the Deal fishing boat *Spartan* to

The tide turns in favour of the Fishermen

raise a team. The game began at 5 p.m. after the sides had followed the tide out. They carried on until sunset when the fishermen clinched the match.

Cahir Park were playing Constitution in a Munster Cricket Union encounter. Major 'Spear' Nolan, umpiring at square leg, suddenly appealed against the light, or rather, the lack of it. The appeal was directed at the two captains, one of whom was batting and the other keeping wicket. Both unanimously rejected the peremptory suggestion, whereupon the affronted Major stalked from the field to the accompaniment of catcalls and 'the stentorian tones of his fellow officer, Paddy Pole-Carew, giving biographical and historical descriptions of earlier unmarried members of the Nolan family'.

> 'Whenever I look down the wicket at the batsman I see a geezer trying to ruin my career. I'm not going to let that happen, am I?'
>
> Phil Tufnell

In 1963, Bob Ascough, playing for Stavely, scored a century against Minskip, although suffering the disability of having no left arm from the elbow downwards.

Charles Bulpett, who sometimes played cricket under the pseudonym 'CW Lloyd', backed himself for £200 to walk a mile, run a mile and ride a mile in 18 minutes. Having won the bet, he was encouraged to increase the stake the following year, 1888.

This time for a bet of £1000 to £400 he repeated his success within 16 and a half minutes.

AJ Fleming, a stylish batsman with the Leinster Club in Ireland a century or so ago, always wore an eyeglass which he found it necessary to remove and wipe after every ball. Bowlers used to become so exasperated by the delay that their bowling sometimes went to pieces.

Leslie Cohen, coming on to bowl against Chalfont St Peter, was asked by the umpire what he was about to deliver. 'Alternate left and right arm over,' was the reply. And that is what he proceeded to do.

Three years after the Battle of Waterloo and just before the conclusion of the Allied Occupation, the Duke of Wellington rode on horseback to see a cricket match at Cambrai. Just over a quarter of a century before, as a junior officer, he had played cricket for All-Ireland.

General Sir Miles Dempsey, who commanded the Second Army in the 1944 invasion of Normandy, was a slow left-arm bowler and capable batsman who played twice for Sussex in 1919.

William Fryer took up umpiring – successfully – having lost the sight of one eye.

Formerly, he had played for twenty years from 1852 as a fine wicket-keeper and hard-hitting batsman. It was in September 1862 that he became blind in the right eye having been thrown from a trap. He continued to bat well for Kent, though thereafter seldom kept wicket. In 1864, he took 8 wickets for 40 runs in an innings against England at Lord's.

The Arrael Griffin Colliery team failed to turn up for a match one Saturday afternoon because they were stuck 500 feet below ground after a shift. The cage carrying them to the surface had broken down.

Sir Andrew Scott, who had played for the county of Nairn, was prone to be dismissed in one of two ways: either lbw or run out. In an attempt to offset the former, he would practise with a stump attached to the offending limb, his right leg. Regarding the latter, he was described as 'when once started he tore up the pitch like a dray horse coming home for his oats in the evening'.

At Glascold, the railway line intersected the playing area. Innings were interrupted to let the train through.

Extract from a speech given by Dudley Marsden at the 1975 Annual Dinner of Exmouth Cricket Club:'The Gear Steward reported the loss of 5 right-footed pads, 2 left-handed wicket-keeping gloves, 2 stumps and one bail. The police have produced identikit pictures and are searching for 5 left-handed batsmen, one ambidextrous wicket-keeper with a frost-bitten left hand and one crippled defendant out on bail.'

> 'He was wearing an expression of permanent pained bewilderment "like a man who's just stepped into a lift-shaft". The riposte followed – a sumptuous square-cut which unfolded like a royal carpet all the way to the boundary.'
> Michael Henderson on David Gower (Derbys. v Leics. 1988),
> *The Guardian*

> 'Chris Cowdrey was a victim of the strange year in Test cricket, when the selectors decided to give every cricketer in England who had not so far captained England a chance to do so.'
> Miles Kington,
> *The Independent*

Norman Vere Grace, the fifth son of EM 'The Coroner', once took all ten wickets in an innings, two of them in the final over and the tenth with the last ball.

A slow bowler, he apparently had a very similar action to his uncle WG. He played for Thornbury, the club reformed in 1871 with his father as captain, secretary and treasurer. NV Grace was a captain in the Navy and represented the service on three occasions against the Army at Lord's and in many other parts of the world.

On one occasion during a county game, WG Grace made a towering hit into the outfield. As he was turning for his second run, he saw that a fielder was in position under the ball so he straight away declared the innings closed. Grace then persuaded the umpire into giving him not out on the grounds that the catch was made after the declaration.

Sylvia 'Swin' Swinburne, of the Redoubtables Women's Cricket Club and also captain of Zwaafians, started cricket in every station to which she was posted as a Squadron Officer during World War Two. Chairwoman of the Women's Cricket Association from 1971 to 1977, she masterminded the first ever World Cup Competition in 1973, when England beat Australia in the final at Edgbaston. It was also through her initiative that the England Women's side played at Lord's for the first time.

Two men were overheard conversing on a tram in Seaton, Devon. One did all the talking:
'No, Bill didn't get much out of his day's cricket. 'E had to pay eight bob for his railway fare, and lost 'is day's screw and was fined a shilling for being late next morning, and 'e didn't get no wickets, and 'e missed four ketches, and 'e got a couple of bootiful blobs. 'E did feel sold, 'e did.'

'Other-End' Brown used to play for Thornbury at the same time as 'The Little Doctor', EM Grace. Apparently, Brown was a great character; he had to be, for his cricketing contributions were minimal. Brown never bowled, batted negligibly and seldom fielded cleanly. Nevertheless, when the ball was in his hands 'it would be returned to the wicket with unerring aim and amazing speed'.

It is reported that EM, in trepidation that his bowling hand would be injured by these lightning throw-ins, would shout: 'T'other end, Brown!', which, of course, is how he came by the nickname.

Brown could throw a ball 100 yards and more while standing in a tub!

Tom Emmett, prototype of the great characters of Yorkshire cricket down the years, was captain of the county for five years before handing over in 1883 to Martin (later Lord) Hawke. They were a wayward team in those days, their fielding poor, as Emmett, a left-arm fast bowler, knew only too well.

'What's the team like, Tom?' asked Hawke, on his appointment. 'Well, Mr Hawke,' replied Tom with more than a touch of acidity, 'there's an epidemic in this team. But don't fret hersen, sir. It isn't catching.'

The 'Society for the Improvement of Things in General and the Diffusion of Perfect Equality' proposed that WG Grace 'shall be declared out whenever the umpire likes', or alternatively 'shall not be allowed to play at all'. This motion was in 1873.

The famous Doctor earned a large amount of money from playing cricket although ostensibly an amateur. Arriving at Lord's by cab one day, as was his practice, he told the driver to see the secretary of the MCC about the fare. The secretary was fed up with the demands of WG and told the driver to go back to Grace and ask him for the money. Grace was half-undressed in the changing-room when the driver put his head round the door, and became very tight-lipped when he heard the relayed message.

Immediately, he put his braces and jacket on and drove off home in the cab. The MCC always paid his fare after that!

Bunny Tattersall, wicket-keeper for I Zingari, was wounded in the First World War, the result of which was one artificial leg. On the first evening of a two-day game in South Hampshire in 1926, he discovered that it had broken. There was no recourse but to motor 90 miles home and 90 miles back again to fetch a spare leg before the next day's play.

Before the First World War, Blackheath's wicket-keeper was the local postman, Frank Chitty, who used to take to the field with a batsman's pad worn underneath his shirt. Chitty suffered from a limp and had only one eye.

Tattersall, a wicket-keeper who needed a fine leg

48

'Either he's signalling one short or there's a plane about to land'

In 1945, two RAF teams played trial matches on a matting wicket laid out on a concrete runway at Teheran. A really good straight drive could sometimes travel for about 600 yards, whereas any firm shot to the covers or mid-wicket would pull up within 35. It was essential to keep an eye on the control tower for incoming aircraft. Inevitably, on one occasion nobody did, until the controller was espied frantically tearing towards the runway waving his shirt. An aircraft was making its final circuit. Never was cricket terminated so quickly.

WG Grace breaks the ice with a century

WG Grace played on a frozen lake at Windsor Park one winter in the 1870s. A couple of fielders fell through the ice in their efforts to stop WG scoring a resolute century.

The second Earl of Leicester, Thomas William Coke, was born in 1822 and died in 1907 in his 87th year. An able cricketer, he played for Norfolk and was President of the MCC and Father of the House of Lords. It is perhaps the only time that one person has held the top office in two distinguished arenas barely three miles apart bearing the same name – albeit one minus the apostrophe.

Leicester's genealogy was similarly convoluted. 'He survived the birth of his father by no fewer than 155 years; he had a half-sister who married as far back as 1794; and he married for the second time in 1875, exactly a century after his father's marriage. His eldest son was born in 1848 and his youngest in 1893.' Leicester is also credited with one hundred on the field of play.

It was said that Arthur Jones owed his batting position 'next to the roller' in the Lloyd's Register CC to laughing at the wrong time. One day his skipper, CS Mabey, had made a miraculous but, in fact, very fortuitous catch. He had put up his right hand to take the ball though it actually lodged in his left hand, which was dangling by his side. Mabey quickly explained that the poised right hand had been shielding the sun from his eyes! Jones was seen to be doubled up on the ground totally convulsed with tears running down his face.

In the 1902 match between Beddington and London County, the umpire gave Grace not out when he was caught by the Revd HA Hodgson in the slips.

'Well, Rector, I shall not give you another chance,' said WG.

The very next ball he edged straight to the Rector, who was so surprised that he dropped it!

The Leicestershire batsman AE Knight was of a religious bent. He had a habit of praying on bended knee at the crease before starting his innings. This time-consuming ritual infuriated the Lancashire fast bowler Walter Brearley who was easily riled.

After casting a derisory look at the kneeling Knight, he complained to the umpire about 'unfair assistance'.

Jake Madden, a pro at the Workington Club, was a bruising batsman and a stock bowler who could turn the ball both ways. A real 'character', he was a lamplighter in the winter. Asked how to play slow bowling, Madden replied: 'Git oot and lamm it afore it lets.'

In pre-Beeching days a railway line ran alongside the cricket ground at Great Alne in Warwickshire. During one Saturday game a ball was hit through the window of a passing train – and thrown back again by the guard on its return journey two hours later.

> 'On the first day, Logie decided to chance his arm and it came off.'
> Trevor Bailey, Radio 3

The Revd FH Gillingham, of Essex and broadcasting fame, noticed a single spectator in the pavilion during the annual fixture at the Oval between the Clergy of South London and the Clergy of North London. Thinking that the man deserved commendation, Gillingham approached and thanked him for taking such an interest in the poor class of cricket played by the clergy. The man's reply was: 'Oh, I don't come here to watch the cricket. This is the only place I know in London where the bar is open all day.'

On 20 May 1905, *The Black and White Illustrated Budget* displayed on the front cover a photograph of towering Monty Noble, 'the Colonial Vice-Captain, and Smaun Sing Hpoo, the smallest cricketer in the world'.

The diminutive Hpoo was no taller than Noble's bat which he was helping to hold.

The only flat part of a field at Tredunmock was a footpath which sometimes served as a pitch. The fielders were calf-high in long grass, buttercups and daisies.

'Partridge, unaware of gaming season limitations, had not yet entered full flight but was obviously awaiting the entry of Brian Whale to the attack. He then batted with consummate relish and, although he used a few unorthodox parts of the bat, he did indeed awake the slumbers of the scorer, Elaine Norsworthy, to induce frantic activity which did not cease until 4 a.m. next morning, when she gave birth to her first, a bouncing daughter.'
Match report, Woking News-Mail, 20 September 1979

Mrs S Nettur, a teacher, was the official scorer for the Brunei State Cricket Association and accompanied the touring side to Singapore in 1972.

In a match at Cranford during the 1957 season, a strong off-drive struggled to reach the boundary and then vanished. Eventually, it was found to have dropped down a hole made to hold a perimeter post. In order to retrieve the ball, a spade had to be found and the hole enlarged.

The Revd Arthur Butler, captain of Rugby cricket in the late 1840s, is said to have been the only man to have jumped the River Cherwell, a tributary of the Thames at Oxford.

Edward Rae's claim to a place in the obituary columns of *Wisden's Almanack* rests solely on his introduction of cricket into Russian Lapland.

John Lewis Byrom was so fanatical about the game that advertisements for a job at his Friarmere Mill in 1881 read: 'Finisher required. Must be a good left-hand batsman.'

Hampshire journeyed to Leyton to play Essex on 28 May 1888, only to find no opposition . . . the date had been altered and the Essex secretary had forgotten to inform his Hampshire counterpart.

Sir Barnes Wallis, most widely remembered as the inventor of the 'bouncing bomb' of Dambuster fame, once contacted the cricket authorities and offered to design a cricket ball which, undetected, would be unplayable by any batsman. Apparently, they were horrified.

In a game of the Rottingdean CC played on Beacon Hill, a batsman, on the point of receiving his first ball, stood back and held up his hand. In response to questioning stares, he said that a sailing ship was passing behind the bowler's arm.

At Fountains Abbey three sticks were placed in the ground to represent the Holy Trinity. This 'wicket' was guarded in turn by eleven monks representing the faithful apostles. Armed with clubs they defended the Kingdom of Heaven against the Devil, in this case another monk who bowled with a wooden ball. There was no need for umpires as God answered every appeal.

Frederick Hyland played once for Hampshire, as a professional in 1924, in a game reduced by rain to only two overs during which Northants made 1 for 0. It has been conjectured that in Hyland's first-class career he did not ever touch the ball.

William Carter, who played for Surrey, was employed as a private detective by the Jockey Club after his cricketing days were over.

Percy De Paravicini was an all-rounder *par excellence*, the sort who specialised in everything. At football, he played for Cambridge University and England and in two FA Cup Finals for Old Etonians, picking up a winner's medal against Blackburn Rovers in 1882. At cricket, he played as a middle-order batsman, slow bowler and splendid fielder for Cambridge again, a blue in all four years, for Buckinghamshire and Middlesex. In a minor match with literally a minute or so to go and fifteen runs required, he strode to the wicket, hit the first ball for eight and the second for seven!

Kenneth Gandar Dower was one of the most remarkable all-rounders of all time. A scholar of Trinity, editor of *The Granta*, a fine orator at the Union, he represented Cambridge University at six games: lawn tennis, real tennis, squash, Eton fives, Rugby fives and billiards, becoming British Amateur Champion at three of them.

Roy Yglesias, who played cricket with Dower, recalls: 'Gandar was a most creative player; twice he nearly achieved the high lob which lands on the bails (a type of bowling immortalised by Arthur Conan Doyle in his tale about "Spedegues Dropper"). He had what is now called a deadpan expression, and could appeal in a serious whisper to the umpire before, during or after his actual deliveries. He would try to confuse fieldsmen by arranging with his batting partner to call "no" when he meant "yes" and "yes" when he meant "no". Remarkably few run-outs ensued, but much mirth . . . He tried to introduce cheetah-racing at the White City but it never took on. He flew in the King's Cup and wrote a book called *The Spotted Lion*. He was a war correspondent and lost his life at sea in 1942.'

The recently appointed director of Christians in Sport, the Revd

Every bowler's nightmare

Andrew Wingfield-Digby, used to captain Dorset. Once in a game against Cheshire he ordered the bowling of more than 50 wides to encourage the opposition to go for a win. Which commandment did he break?

Directions on an old bottle of 'Rubitine', discovered in a Northamptonshire barn, read: 'Applied to Rubber-Faced Gauntlets, the Preparation gives the perfect tackiness all Wicket-Keepers desire.'

Playing for Hounslow Congs CC in 1957, John Lavers must have felt that fate was not on his side. During one over, he was twice no-balled by the square-leg umpire for alleged throwing and then hit the stumps only to find that the bail had become wedged between the uprights and the batsman was given not out.

Joel Woolf Barnato, who played six matches for Surrey between 1928 and 1930 as a wicket-keeper, was better known as a long-distance racing driver. He was the son of diamond merchant Barney Barnato.

Peter Cazalet, who opened the innings for Oxford University and Kent, was also a steeplechase jockey and later, for a quarter of a century, in charge of the Queen Mother's horses.

As many as eight or nine games being played at the same time during weekends can be seen on some of London's extensive parklands, commons and playing-fields. The boundaries for these matches are mostly ill-defined and often a ball from one game ends up in the middle of another.

Peter Mahoney, who founded his own team for parks competition in the 1950s, recalls one occasion in which two fielders converged under catches from two games and both caught the 'wrong' ball.

In 1978, Eddie Johnson at the age of 74 completed a golden jubilee playing for two clubs: 50 years for his Saturday side, North Leeds, and 50 years with Leeds Allerton, whose friendly encounters took place only on Wednesdays.

The immortal Wilfred Rhodes, taking part in a charity game and fending off fiery deliveries from a sweating, aspiring, young fast bowler, called out: 'Who a' they cum to see, thee or me?'

Matches at the Victoria Barracks, Windsor, called for adaptations to the rules. Regarding boundaries, four was given for a broken window, any shot clearing the barracks to off or leg and for a drive into the Colonel's favourite flower bed. A hit through a corridor which led to the latrines was a six, provided it reached its ultimate goal.

A middle-order batsman and right-arm medium pace bowler who played for Sussex and Warwickshire and football for West Bromwich Albion? Of course, it can only be John Major.

As AC MacLaren, England Test captain, moved into position to catch a cloud-splitting skier from an Australian batsman, the latter shouted out in desperation: 'Miss it, Archie, and you can kiss me big sister!'

In an XI of England versus XIV of Hampshire encounter played in September 1848, play was resumed on the second day at 7 o'clock in the morning.

It has been said that everything in cricket has happened at Eton Wick; in fact, some of it has happened before cricketers even arrived there. John Ritchie, stopping in the bar of a well-known City tavern on his journey across London to the ground, demonstrated to a team-mate his rarely-called-upon bowling action. In so doing, he accidentally tipped the full beer glass being held by another customer straight through the pub window into Fleet Street. Apparently, full reparations were made, with Ritchie now convinced that his bowling would be more in demand.

'Hurl' Humphries, the Somerset cricketer, had a reputation as the fastest thrower in the West. It is reported that he regularly ran out batsmen embarking on their first run from his position at *long off*. It was not unknown for bowlers to be knocked off their feet by the velocity of returns that arrived on the long hop.

> After having spent a fruitless morning bowling to Hobbs and Sandham at the Oval, R Robertson-Glasgow, also known as 'Crusoe', on Hobbs: 'It's like bowling to God on concrete.'

James Verity, grandson of Hedley, the great Yorkshire and England slow left-arm bowler, has represented Wales at under-15 level, as an opening batsman.

Richard Johnson, batting for the Jesters Cricket Club against Totteridge in 1975, hit a six onto a spectator's car; the owner, who was lying on the grass nearby with a lady companion, sprang angrily to his feet, whereupon his trousers fell down!

Captain Charles Cumberland, renowned fast bowler for Kent and All-England in the late eighteenth century, was a member of the White Conduit Club – the forebear of MCC – and the son of the dramatist, essayist and secret service agent, Richard Cumberland. Charles was one of the first to present a hat as a measure of achievement to individuals of a team.

A schoolmistress, who played for a Ladies' XI near Swindon, was always correctly attired with an ankle-length dress. Whenever the ball came in her direction she would jump over it and then give chase – which provided much amusement for onlookers.

Her actions did have a hidden asset, however, in that by the time the ball was retrieved the batswomen were often exhausted from running and therefore more easily dismissed.

The Warwickshire secretary noticed that at the end of the first day's play in a county match, a spectator was copying all the details from the scoreboard. The following morning he was there again checking the numbers. The same thing happened at the end of the second day's play and on the morning of the third. When asked to explain, it transpired he was an American who was proving to his own satisfaction that 'this really was a three-day ball game'.

Cricket has been suggested as one possible antidote to AIDS. A recent letter-writer to the *Bangkok Times* took the view that 'cricket-playing nations are capable of only limited amounts of sexual activity'.

'Who told him it was just like polo with a different bat?'

The Prince of Wales scored 4 not out off four balls from 11-year-old Luke MacDonald in a knockabout game when opening the indoor school for the Arundel Castle Cricket Foundation in August 1991. Twenty-three years earlier he had reached 20, including a six and two fours, for Lord Brabourne's XI in a charity match against a grand prix drivers' side at Ashford, Kent. On that occasion, the Prince was out to a catch by Bruce McLaren off the bowling of Graham Hill.

On the public address was commentator Raymond Baxter: 'Charles has scored two so far. Oh, I'm terribly sorry, that should be six. Chaps have been put in the Bloody Tower for less.'

One of the most popular comedy talk shows on Pakistan TV, 'Studio 2½', was closed down after an item was shown ridiculing the selectors who had omitted Shoaib Mohammad from the national side which won the Sharjah Tournament. It was felt the programme displayed ethnic prejudice.

It was a case of drunk, but not disorderly, at a match on Dartford Brent in 1834. The encounter was between millwrights and engineers employed at the local Hall's engineering works. They had

Bowled over by Mr Crosby's ale

been given a 'most capital and substantial hot dinner' together with a plentiful supply of extremely strong wine courtesy of Mr Crosby from The Coach and Horses.

Most of the players afterwards found themselves 'so heady' that they were unable to field except on all fours!

EH Budd, one of the most famous all-rounders of the nineteenth century, in a match against twenty-two of Nottingham in 1817, caught nine men. He had also demonstrated his colossal striking powers by hitting a nine, all run, at the Dorset Square ground some years earlier.

Much to Budd's chagrin, the proprietor, Thomas Lord, who had promised a substantial reward to anyone who proved his ground too small, refused to pay.

Budd's displeasure was again in evidence in 1850 when, as a veteran in a game between Purton and Marlborough College, three of his deliveries were struck over the boundary successively by a schoolboy, one EJ Gayer.

When the ball was returned to Budd, he dashed it to the ground, growled that 'such swiping wasn't the game' and refused to bowl another over.

By tradition, Leicestershire CC has a dinner for the last match of the season whether it involves the First or Second XI. In 1991, the Second XI were scheduled to play Sussex at Hove between 11 and 13 September. Leicestershire bowled out Sussex for 213 on the first day and then scored 479 for 4 by the end of the second. That evening the team went out to a Chinese restaurant for dinner. The next day seven of the eleven players went down with food poisoning. Before abandoning the match, there was hurried consultation with the TCCB who gave permission to do so.

At a rustic venue in Ireland the uniform of the local team consisted of white shirt and cap, navy-blue trousers and brown boots. Many of the spectators were similarly garbed and one of these wandered on to the field when a ball was lofted towards the boundary and took a spectacular catch.

At the same time, an 'official' fielder on the far side of the ground quickly disappeared into the crowd.

One-time President of the MCC, Lord Cobham, batting for the Band of Brothers against Bluemantles, was elated when his hit for six cleared the pavilion at Tunbridge Wells. The sound of shattering glass served as a kind of accolade for the stroke. It was only later, when returning to his car, that he found the windscreen in smithereens.

> 'Alan Green, the occasional off-spinner, might just turn a spin-drier, but not much else.'
> Mihir Bose, *Sunday Times*

Women's league cricket in Denmark is keenly contested. During one match at Køge, the new arrival at the crease demanded a runner. 'Why?' she was asked. 'Are you injured?'

'No,' replied the batswoman, 'but I'm pregnant.'

After consultation, her claim was rejected because it was said that her incapacity had not occurred whilst the game was in progress.

During the middle of the last century, the Railway Company took over land adjoining the Whitehaven Cricket Club. The club members complained of engines that emitted dirt and sooty smoke and particularly of drivers and firemen who shouted ribald comments. The recipient of the letter of protest to the Railway Company was Mr I Will. Belch.

THE RULE
THAT PROVES THE
EXCEPTION

With cricket, it often seems that no sooner has an exceptional feat been achieved than another occurs which is just as good or even better . . .

Question Who made a century without running at all throughout the innings?
Answer Robert Hamilton Lambert, who in 1893 when only 19 scored 115 for JM Meldon's touring team v Laverton's XI at Westbury, Wiltshire. Owing to injury Lambert had a runner and, in fact, he did not field at any stage of the match.

Lambert became the WG Grace of Irish cricket – a prolific and devastatingly effective all-rounder, he shared a common birthday with the great man, who said of him: 'How do you improve on perfection?' An international over three decades, he also once turned out for Scotland and, similarly, London County. He achieved a century of centuries including eight double centuries and the double (1000 runs and 100 wickets) in nine consecutive seasons. In 1895, he amassed 248 not out in 125 minutes for Leinster v Fitzwilliam (the first 100 in 40 minutes) and 8 for 23. Later that summer he achieved a hat-trick in each innings for Stedalt v Lord Louth's team and at the end of the season had accumulated 2040 runs and 209 wickets. He was a member of Leinster Club for 67 years who, in their brochure, give Lambert's batting average as 217!

Schoolmaster Billy Hyman, batting for Bath Association against Thornbury on the 'Ship' ground in July 1902, scored an incredible 359 not out in 100 minutes, mostly off the bowling of EM Grace. Other bowlers punished were the Gloucester trio, Sellick, Spry and Paish.

The Bath team had journeyed to the match by coach and four plus a trumpeter. 'They batted first and scored 124 to which Thornbury replied with 85. The Bath second innings began at 4.35 and when stumps were drawn at 6.25 the score was 461 for 6 wickets, a scoring rate of something like four runs per minute!' Six balls were used during the onslaught and tactfully no bowling analysis was kept of the second innings.

Four years later, Grace established his own 350 niche when he took 352 wickets in the season.

Ernie Tagg bowling for Sutton v Marlow Brewery in 1936 took all 10 for 14 runs. Every one of his victims was bowled.

The result of a game in India as reported by the *New Times* in 1922 caused some perplexity. It stated that the Europeans of Railway Shed scored 38½ runs with four players absent and their opponents, the Union Club of Rohri, managed 39½ runs with five wickets in hand. Where did the half runs come from?

Billy Poll took four catches at slip for Adel in 1938 – standing next to him in the gully was his son Bruce, who took five. All were in the same innings.

One of the most exciting recoveries in club cricket took place in April 1954 in a game between South Devon and Exmouth. Exmouth dismissed their opponents for what seemed a meagre 104, only to lose nine wickets for 20 in reply against the tricky leg-spin bowling of Tom Dean, once of Hampshire. The captain of Exmouth, John Dilks, going in at no. 10, was joined by schoolboy Howard Royston. In the next 45 minutes, Dilks with a great array of strokes scored 71 whilst Royston defended stoutly for 3 not out.

With only 4 required for victory, however, Dilks was beaten by a ball from Dean who finished with 9 for 34. A case of glorious defeat snatched from the jaws of victory.

The Sion Mills Company ground in Co. Tyrone was the scene of one of the biggest upsets in cricket history in 1969. The local factory closed at midday in order to let the workforce, in a one-street town of some 1600 souls, see Ireland take on the mighty West Indies. But by 12.30, the leprechauns had skittled out their opponents for 25 runs and then later passed their total for the loss of one wicket. At one stage, West Indies were 8 for 6 and then 12

for 9. After completing their nine-wicket victory in the one-day game, Ireland continued batting and declared 100 runs ahead in order to let the crowd see the tourists bat.

In a match at Lampton Park in 1957, Tony Evans went in with one ball of the over left to play to prevent a hat-trick. From that ball he scored a single and therefore faced the first ball of the next over from which he also had to prevent a hat-trick. There must be few precedents for the same batsman being called upon to stop two hat-tricks with two consecutive balls.

Pride was paramount in a Birmingham League encounter between Old Hill and Moseley. Batting on a sodden pitch, Moseley stumbled to 16 for 9 before their captain, Malcolm Eustace, one of seven players out for a duck, declared. 'I didn't want to see a Moseley side all out for under 20,' he explained. Old Hill won by 10 wickets.

In 1979, playing for Curry Rivel, Somerset, against Pitminster, Brian Rostill was hit for 17 runs in his opening eight-ball over. In his next over, he captured six wickets, all clean-bowled. In this second over, he also bowled two no-balls which hit the stumps.

The downs, ups and downs of cricket were never more vividly illustrated than when Adam Seymour had four innings in four

Caught at the wicket then caught in the act

days. On the Sunday, the dreaded nought for Sussex in 'the over 40 bash'; on the Monday, a similar figure for the Second Eleven in the Bain Clarkson Trophy; on the Tuesday, a century for the 2nds v Sussex at Southend, the first day of a three-day match; and on Wednesday, a first-ball duck for the 1sts in a Nat West Trophy tie against Surrey at the Oval. (A new regulation in 1991 allowed Essex to remove Seymour from the game against Sussex, so that he could replace the injured Nadeem Shahid.)

'Cricketing detective Brian Arkle, 34, arrested a pavilion intruder, then returned to catch out the opposition's best batsman and score 105 for Gateshead Fell in their six-wicket win over Durham City.'

The Daily Mail

In beating Queensland by 4 wickets in a Sheffield Shield match at Adelaide in February 1992, South Australia compiled the highest fourth innings winning total in first-class cricket this century. Set 506 to win, they reached the target with two balls to spare. Their total is one run short of the all-time record of 507 for 7 by Cambridge University against MCC and Ground in 1896.

Hussein Manack, a South African student playing for St Michael's CC in Dumfries, scored 148 not out and then took 10 wickets for 11 runs against Melrose in 1991.

Seventeen-year-old Spencer Turnbull scored 258 not out, a Slazenger Surrey League record, for Old Suttonians against Morden Spartans after the doctor had advised him to rest his back for six weeks.

Tom Moody scored the fastest first-class hundred, albeit expedited in the desire for a declaration, with 103 off 36 balls in 26 minutes. He was batting for Warwickshire against Glamorgan at Swansea in 1990.

Twelve-year-old David Sales, a pupil of Cumnor House Preparatory School, Purley, who captained Surrey Under-12s, in five innings in 1991 scored 63 (retired), 102, 111 (retired), 198 not out and 102 (retired). A total of 576 for once out.

For a stake of £5 the eccentric Nottinghamshire batsman George Gunn accepted an offer to take part in a single-wicket match against a local amateur. After Gunn had reached 620 not out, he made it easier for his opponent by allowing him to bowl at a heavy roller instead of the stumps. It made no difference and when Gunn's score stood at 777 the amateur conceded the match.

Reports of other individual scores in the six and seven hundreds have come from Donald Weekes, the West Indian batsman, though they are unsubstantiated, as is C Calleson's score of 610 not out for The Avenue v Alexandra at Melbourne in 1906 which *The Age* noted as including 64 fours, 10 fives, 7 sixes, 1 eight, 1 nine and 1 eleven. AEJ Collins's score of 628 not out at Clifton College in 1899 remains the highest authenticated score in an organised fully complemented match.

After rain had prevented play, it took 78 deliveries at a single stump before Durham beat Leicestershire in a shoot-out to decide the Tilcon Trophy at Harrogate in 1991.

Batting consistency over a long period is a true sign of quality. Alan Marshal, an Australian, who played for several clubs including London County while qualifying for Surrey, scored 4350 runs in all matches in 1906, as well as taking 210 wickets. Joe Misso, with Dutch and Ceylonese antecedents, had, by the time he retired, amassed 354 centuries. The majority were for the Burgher Recreation Club and the Ceylon Cricket Association; 90 were in England for GWR and Brentham CC. Misso's career spread over 38 years and pales somewhat against Jack Hyams' 58 years at the crease, which have produced over 112 000 runs, 168 centuries and 1283 wickets. The most runs Hyams scored in a season was 4328 in 1953. His career batting average is 41.03 and he is the only batsman to score centuries in seven successive decades with 1000-plus runs annually since 1934 – the very same year, incidentally, that Misso, aged fourteen, scored his first ton. Hyams has played in the Yorkshire and Birmingham Leagues and for Stoics, the Forty Club, London Counties and the Magdala Club. He is a retired pet-shop owner.

A game of cricket was played at Newenden, Kent, between five gentlemen of Kent and five gentlemen of Sussex, which terminated as follows:

Kent	First Innings	
Mr G Tolhurst	b Warner	0
Mr T Ayerst	b Warner	0
Mr W Hunson	c Warner	0
Mr R Levett	b Warner	0
Mr S Maynard	lbw	0

Sussex	First Innings	
Mr J Furner	b Ayerst	0
Mr T Edwards	b Ayerst	0
Mr T Coppinger	b Ayerst	0
Mr R Moore	b Ayerst	0
Mr T Warner	b Ayerst	0

Night coming on prevented the second innings being played.
Evans and Ruffy's Farmers' Journal and Agricultural Advertizer,
19 October 1825

In a match between Freshwater and Northwood at Bowes in 1874, a Mr Collins scored 338 runs in little more than three hours. His extraordinary knock was compounded, says *The Field*, of 'one 9, two 7s, six 6s, twelve 5s, twenty-five 4s, seventeen 3s, eighteen 2s and thirty-three singles'. Surely, the composition of the runs makes 339? Ah, well! Who's counting?

In 1825, in what was described as a single-wicket match, Thomas Strange, aged 55, scored 50 and beat a side of six men by an innings and 27 runs on the Common at Tunbridge Wells.

A batsman made 2 in fourteen minutes for Thorne Colliery Nightjars. Whilst he was doing that, his partner, Samuel Harper, was scoring 100.

Lisa Nye, the England Women's wicket-keeper, captured eight dismissals in New Zealand's first innings in the third Test at New Plymouth in 1992. Nye took six catches and two stumpings.

In 1827, a bizarre game between the 'Old Ladies of Southborough' and the 'Young Ladies of Tunbridge Wells' was played for three bottles of gin and three pounds of the best gunpowder tea. The 'Old Ladies' were too sharp for their younger opponents and won easily by 52 runs.

In 1834, a novel attempt to offset disparate ability at cricket took place. Eleven of Nottingham met thirteen of Bingham, the former side having two innings, the latter four. Nottingham won by eight wickets.

Mr Charles Brown of Godmanchester, Huntingdon, took six wickets in six successive balls in 1874. Five of his victims, who played for Willingham in Cambridgeshire, were clean bowled, the other lbw.

In 1900, a game between Huckamore CC and Ulidia CC ended in a tie – 53 each. Strangely, both captains scored 31 and a bowler from each side had the identical analysis of 2 for 3.

S Redgate alone met and defeated eleven of the Kensington Club at Nottingham in 1836. Redgate made 24 in his two innings and the Kensington XI totalled 10.

In 1844, the *Chelmsford Chronicle* reported 'an unexampled feat at cricket'. Mr Jno. Almond playing for Great Bentley 'put out the whole side of the Boxted gentlemen by his own hand by bowling down seven wickets, two catches and stumping one'.

Fred Crawshay, stalwart of the South Oxfordshire Amateurs for many years, displayed his extreme versatility as a bowler by taking six wickets with spin against Wiltshire Queries in 1948 – three with his right hand and three with his left!

In previous encounters against the same side, Crawshay had bowled right-hand away swingers.

Cawood beat Dringhouses in 1979 without scoring a single run from the bat. Dringhouses were dismissed for 2 and then the first ball of the Cawood innings went for 4 byes.

There were fourteen lbw decisions in the third Test between Pakistan and Sri Lanka at Faisalabad in January 1992 – a world record for Tests. The first-class record is nineteen lbw dismissals – out of 33 wickets to fall, Patiala v Delhi, 1953/54 season.

Gravesend CC's Glen Biddings, an Australian, hit six 6s in an over off G Harris of Ardleigh Green Wednesday XI in September 1991. Giddings eventually completed a century, his last 50 coming off just twelve balls.

In 1909, A Carton de Wiart, playing at Brighton for the Officers of the 4th Dragoon Guards against the Sergeants' Mess, took 7 for 0 in 11 balls, having just retired after scoring 102.

ON YER WAY!

What is it that makes a man want to umpire? Very few have an inclination to change the course of history; indeed, very few want to alter the future. Yet careers and livelihoods have been altered irretrievably by that finger pointing towards the sky. It has its funny side, of course – a man in a white coat standing behind three sticks in the middle of a field on a hot afternoon with thick sweaters wrapped around his middle and over his shoulders, transferring pebbles from one pocket to the other . . . It's called an occupation. The hazards have to be read to be believed . . .

Misfortune for Mr Collins at Southampton

Mr Collins, batting for Odd Fellows against Southampton Union Club in 1856, struck the ball only for his bat to break in two. He still retained the handle but the remainder of the bat had knocked down his wicket. The umpire signalled 'not out', whereupon the Southampton stumper appealed to the other official. The response was unequivocal: 'Out, decidedly.' The conflict of opinion was resolved by Collins retiring gracefully to the pavilion.

Alfred Isaac Russell, keeping wicket for Hampshire against Essex, was overly enthusiastic after taking a catch behind the stumps. He threw the ball into the air and appealed vociferously. 'Not out,' said the umpire, 'I won't be rushed.'

One umpire, in a game involving Cheam CC in 1899, refused to give a batsman out to what had obviously been a catch. Responding to indignant looks from the fielders, he said: 'You were too slow in appealing.'

In a schools match in Wales, Test umpire Emrys Davies made a note that there were 52 appeals in each innings. Only four were successful.

Of Beaulieu's match at Boldre in 1889 it was written: '. . . resulted in a win for Boldre by three runs, though with fair play the match would have finished otherwise.

The Boldre umpire in their innings four times disallowed legal claims, and after one of them sagely remarked: "Well, if he hit 'un he's out."'

From *The Athlete*, June 1890:
Sympathetic old lady: 'Why is that little boy crying?'
Small boy: 'He was kicked by three big boys who were playing cricket.'
Sympathetic old lady: 'Did he do anything to the big boys to make them kick him?'
Small boy: 'No. He was just umpiring the game, that's all.'

The umpire Ted Langham was known as the 'joker in the white coat'. A long drive which looked as if it would not quite reach the boundary, in fact, did. The batsman had run three. Ted signalled one short!

Throughout the years, umpires have pleaded with players not to burden them with assorted paraphernalia such as sweaters, caps, money, keys and so on. It is reported that recently jokester Allan Lamb, on going in to bat, persuaded umpire 'Dickie' Bird to look after his portable 'phone by saying that he was expecting an extremely urgent call. Unbeknown to Bird, the twelfth man in the pavilion had been primed to ring at the most inconvenient time, just as the bowler was coming into bowl. Apparently, poor 'Dickie' was caught in three minds: whether to stop the bowler, to answer the call or to ignore the audible and persistent ringing.

A late call from the batsman reaches umpire Dickie Bird

RING RING

'As chairman of the
disciplinary committee I
hereby administer to myself
a slap on the wrist . . .'

When Saddleworth Cricket
League chairman John Bacon
remonstrated with the umpires
over a decision about bad light,
he was reported to the League for
'unbecoming conduct'. Presiding
over the next meeting, he duly
reprimanded himself.

At Storrington in Sussex, Brown
snicked the ball through the slips
and started to run. The ball just

reached the boundary before the
fieldsman and the umpire at the
bowler's end signalled four, but
only after he had received a
confirmatory wave from the
fielders that the ball had indeed
managed to reach the ropes.

By this time the ball had been
returned to the wicket-keeper,
who had taken the bails off and
appealed, with Brown not yet
having returned to the crease.
The square-leg umpire raised his
finger. Brown protested that the

umpire at the bowler's end had signalled a boundary.

'Ah,' said the square-leg umpire, 'he is in charge of his end of the field and I am in charge of mine and I say you are out.'

In the scorebook, Brown is down as having scored a boundary and been run out off the same ball.

Bob Russell once hit a ball into the big elm whose branches overlapped the boundary. It remained in sight and therefore the umpire would not call 'Lost ball'. Eight runs were scored by the perspiring batsmen before a fieldsman retrieved it, whereupon the umpire said: 'Out. The ball has not touched the ground!'

Reaching for a catch

One umpire to another: 'As far as neutral umpires are concerned, I'm better qualified than most. My maternal grandfather was Swiss.'

Rex Audley

In the Victorian era, crowds at matches between Bacup and Haslingdon tended to be excessively partisan. It led to great tension on the field. On one occasion, the Haslingdon umpire, Mr G Whittle, gave a run-out decision against the Bacup professional, Myers. There was much booing, counter-cheering and shouting for the match to be discontinued. After Myers had returned to the pavilion, it was nearly five minutes before the Bacup captain emerged, consulted with Whittle, who then stepped down before the game resumed with a fresh umpire.

Epitaph on an over-obliging umpire:
> When Harry died, they heard him say:
> 'At last I'm free from fetters.
> I'd rather bear six feet of clay
> Than thirteen ruddy sweaters!'

AA Robertson

Just as the bowler was in the act of delivering the ball, Henry Cotterell, the umpire, snorted 'Haugghrfrroi!!' Harold George, the batsman, heaved at the ball – missed and was bowled. He made no move towards the pavilion. 'Howzat?' queried the bowler. 'Out,' responded Cotterell, who then explained that he had not called 'no ball' but that a fly had got into his throat.

Some of the early matches of the Findon Club were played on the North Park of Findon Place at the invitation of Colonel WG Margesson. It was during one of these invitation matches that the umpire, a retired coachman to the Marchioness of Bath and an inveterate humorist, gave guard to a batsman who was holding his bat wide of the leg stump. The umpire called 'Hovel' twice before the batsman realised that he was being given a mark in direct line with the Butcher's Croft Hovel, just outside the perimeter of the ground.

In a club match, the bowler had been rapping the batsman's pads repeatedly and had exercised his lungs on each occasion without success. After seven overs, he stopped by the umpire on his way back to his mark and said somewhat apologetically: 'I hope you don't mind all these appeals, but I'm trying to impress the skipper.'

The umpire is never wrong, or is he? Glynde opening bat, Roger Martin, was much perturbed at being given out caught behind when he knew that he had not got a touch. In the bar after the game the offending umpire, without remorse, admitted to his victim: 'I knew straight away I was wrong, but I thought, "Bugger it, it's done now."'

A two-day match was being played at Whitehaven in Cumberland. On the first day the home side had fared badly and when play resumed on the second morning their opponents looked well set for victory. The local umpire, however, with a series of wayward decisions, soon changed the situation. And then, to everybody's astonishment, he turned down a confident appeal against the last man. 'Why did you do that?' asked a fielder. 'Well, if I'd given 'im out, they wouldn't a' stayed to loonch, and my pa does the caterin',' was the reply.

> 'The essence, the aristocracy of 0 is that it should be surrounded by large scores, that it should resemble the little silent breadwinner in a bus full of fat, noisy women. Indeed, when the years have fixed it in its place, so far from being merely the foil for jewels, it should itself grow, in the fond eye of memory, to the shape and stature of a gem.'
>
> R Robertson-Glasgow

The Amersham umpire was also the parish clerk and one Sunday when the vicar, the Revd ET Drake, a fine lob bowler, came to the end of a prayer, instead of saying 'Amen', he called out 'Over'.

The umpire, Tom Laroche, gave a batsman out, caught at the wicket. The batsman knew he had not touched the ball and stood his ground, arguing. Said Tom: 'That'll teach you to tuck in your straps.'

At Scotby near Carlisle the umpire standing at square-leg instinctively threw up his right hand as protection against a fierce hook from the batsman. The resulting brilliant catch and spontaneous 'Howzat!' from the fielding side were, of course, to no avail. His fellow umpire firmly rejected the appeal and awarded the batsman four runs.

Haslingdon were playing Rochdale. Tom Smith took a brilliant catch behind the stumps. Dick Bentley, the Haslingdon umpire, was so excited that he temporarily forgot his station and exclaimed 'How's that?' 'Out,' replied wicket-keeper Smith, imperturbably passing sentence on his captive.

Many members of the Pembroke Cricket Club in Dublin remember to their cost the umpire who 'prowled the streets of the city all winter extracting various sums of money from hibernating cricketers'. The length of their stay at the wicket in the following season was in direct ratio to the amount contributed.

Harry Mason was bowling for Eynsford. 'Chingy' Hussey was fielding at point and Gordon Wood was batting for Farningham. Gordon played the ball on to his foot and Harry shouted, 'How's that, for lbw?' 'Not out,' replied George 'Yorkie' Robinson who was umpiring. 'Not out?' questioned Harry with a glare. 'Not out,' repeated 'Yorkie'. In fact, Gordon was out, for the ball had skidded off his foot to be caught by 'Chingy' at point. But as 'Yorkie' told Harry with a chuckle afterwards, if he had not added lbw his appeal would have been successful.

Henry Jupp, 'Young Stonewall' for Surrey and England, the soundest of batsmen, appeared once at his native Dorking in a local match only to suffer the indignity of being bowled first ball. Jupp calmly replaced the bails and prepared to face the next delivery. 'Ain't you going, Juppy?' the umpire asked. 'No,' replied Jupp, 'not at Dorking I ain't.'

DUDGEON, DISPENSATION AND DESPATCH

Not all is sweetness and light on the cricket field. Anger, accident and *apodosis* can occur very quickly . . .

DUDGEON

In 1722, a match was due to take place between a so-called London Club and Dartford at Islington. The metropolitan side obviously did not fancy their chances and unsuccessfully tried several ruses to get the game cancelled.

Their final ploy was to object to the inclusion in the Dartford team of a short-statured cricketer called Taylor and to insist that he tied one hand behind his back when bowling. Not unexpectedly, Dartford refused to accept the handicap and offered instead to reduce the prize money from a guinea a head to half-a-guinea, to a crown, to half-a-crown – all to no avail.

The Dartfordians journeyed 36 miles in vain.

Rivalry at cricket between the cities of Sheffield and Nottingham a couple of centuries ago was intense and often led to blows.

At one match in Nottingham, a Sheffield batsman called Osguthorpe defied the efforts of the bowlers 'for several hours' till the score reached 50 for 8. The frustrated spectators, including a group of Sherwood Foresters, then started to hamper and harass the immovable Osguthorpe, so much so that the match was abandoned.

Sheffield had their revenge in the return game of 1772 by putting in the visitors, 'tired out with their journey', to bat 'at 6 p.m. on a pitch so sodden and slippery they could neither strike nor run'.

Facing a total of 14 the Yorkshiremen then had coal slack spread on the pitch (even better than sawdust) and thereby gained an easy victory.

During a cricket match at the Artillery Ground in June 1749, a pickpocket was caught, carried into the stable yard of the Pied Horse in nearby Chiswell Street and there ducked in the horse pond before being rolled in a quantity of soot.

> '*Can't stand those fellas, though, who jump on a bowler when he's taken a wicket. It's like assistants at Harrods mobbing a chap when he's sold a tie.*'
> **Henry Cotton**

> '*Personally, I have always looked on cricket as organised loafing.*'
> **William Temple, Archbishop of Canterbury**

Fifteen years later, at 'the great cricket match behind Montague

House, London', a well-dressed spectator had his pocket picked. While the offender was conveyed to the horse pond, some of the mob reckoned the accuser to be the guilty person. He was seized and received a worse ducking.

A match between Sedbergh School and Burnside came to a halt in 1868 after 'foul play'. Sedbergh's suspicions had been aroused when one of their number was given out as having 'hit wicket'. They started to watch the manoeuvres of the stumper 'when he was clearly

seen to kick the bails off with his toe, in Scaife's case'. The result was much argument, no more play and no further games against 'Burneside cads'.

August 1787. Two members of the Royal Family of tender years, the Prince of Wales and the Duke of York, when residing at Kew 'used frequently to amuse themselves at a game of cricket, in the presence of their Royal parents'. One morning the Duke was doing badly and became irritated, a dispute arose and the two children were soon fighting.

Scaife falls victim to the Burneside cad

The King ordered his sentinel to take them in hand and then he and the Queen walked away. Immediately their parents were out of sight the two youngsters escaped the clutches of the sentinel, who had a ten-minute chase before he managed to effect a re-capture and secure his Royal prisoners in the sentry box. Eventually a page brought permission for their discharge.

During a game between Chertsey and Hambledon in 1864 in which five participants were hurt, a gentleman of fortune was taken up by a warrant for a bastard child which caused a great deal of diversion. The gentleman drew his sword on the occasion and afterwards presented a pistol and went off in triumph.

> *'Barring injuries or sexual indiscretions between now and next Thursday, the three other newcomers (Barnett, Russell and Lawrence) seem certain to get the benefit of the Peter May Emporium's Giant 1988 England Cup Sale.'*
> **Matthew Engel, *The Guardian***

Rashid Patel, Indian international left-arm pace bowler, assaulted fellow international Raman Lamba and his partner Ajay Jadeja with a stump during the final of the Inter-Zone tournament for the Duleep Trophy in 1991. The game was between West Zone and North Zone and the flare-up followed an argument over short-pitched bowling. The match was abandoned and North Zone were declared winners by virtue of first-innings lead.

Amos Bartholomew, grounds-man and umpire for 30 years with the Vine Club, 'once fought a navvy who tried to assert his independence by damaging the turf on the Vine (*one of the oldest cricket grounds still in existence*) and after a severe conflict thoroughly vanquished him'.

> *'Some sections of the press can see no difference between a fast bowler swearing and someone shooting the Queen.'*
> **ST Roebuck, 1988**

Cricket faces many hazards, as is evinced by Sydney Platt of Brynyneuadd in a letter to the *North Wales Chronicle* in 1880: 'Owing to an unpardonable piece of carelessness on the part of their secretary, my eleven were kept waiting on the ground for more than two hours; nor did the match commence until some time after the arrival of the Conway eleven, owing to a fight which took place between two of the Club around the ground . . .'

The Editor of the journal *Cricket* was asked to adjudicate in a wrangle between Buckhurst Hill and Moor Hall, near Harlow in Essex, in 1882.

Moor Hall, playing at home, had bowled out their opponents for 134, fielding the usual complement of eleven including a 'lad in a long black coat'. They had reached 100 for 7 in reply when in to bat came a man who had only just arrived at the ground. Under vehement protest from the visitors he was allowed an innings and eventually Moor Hall scraped home as victors.

'May I ask if this kind of thing is allowed?' wrote an indignant

Shattering the peace at Osbaldwick

Mr RL Allport, leading batsman of Buckhurst Hill.

'Why shouldn't it be allowed?' replied an equally indignant captain of Moor Hall. 'Your side had agreed to a substitute for the late arrival who fielded (in his long black coat) throughout the innings. Our assistant secretary had asked the lad to field for him as, owing to a bad hand, he could only bat.'

The Editor of *Cricket* pronounced in favour of Moor Hall, but thought that possibly it was not quite – well, cricket.

People living near the cricket ground at Osbaldwick near York took exception when three lusty sixes shattered not only the peace but also the tiles on a roof, a window and a barbecue in a garden. In the last case, food was sent flying in all directions.

College lecturer Barry Marrison took it upon himself to stage a sit-down protest on the pitch, which prompted a call for the police to intervene. The club apologised and paid for repairs.

In game at Bath in 1903, Ben Vezey, the Box skipper, led his team off the field after the opposing clergyman-captain refused to accept the umpire's decision that he was out.

In trying to play the ball the cleric had fallen over and broken his wicket. The appeal was made to the umpire at the bowler's end who had promptly raised his finger, but the reverend gentleman claimed he had completed the attempted stroke *before* the wicket was knocked askew.

In the ensuing controversy, the clergyman shifted his defensive stance and quoted Law 47, which stated: 'The umpire at the bowler's wicket shall be appealed to before the umpire at the other end in all cases *except that of stumping, hit wicket, etc.*' Therefore, maintained the dog-collar in the doghouse, 'the umpire at the bowler's end should not have been appealed to at all . . .'

Ben Vezey and the Box team were unimpressed, clambered into their horse brake and drove home.

Buckinghamshire were given a police escort to the station after a match against Carmarthenshire at Stradey Park, Llanelli, some 80 or so years ago. They just managed to catch the last train before striking railwaymen blocked the line and rioters blew up ammunition wagons. After the Riot Act had been read, two men were shot by the military and four were killed in explosions. At the end of that season, Carmarthenshire withdrew from the Minor Counties Championship.

> Question: 'Do you feel that the selectors and yourself have been vindicated by this result?'
>
> Answer: 'I don't think the press are vindictive. They can write what they want.'
> Mike Gatting, ITV

Andy Goram, international for Scotland at both football and cricket, was forced to pack away his white flannels when signing as a goalkeeper for Rangers. Two years earlier, his club at the time, Hibernian, had banned him from playing cricket and he was fined for defying the order to play against the touring Australians.

Mrs Goodson's fury knows no boundaries . . .

When the Suffragette movement was at its height, some of its followers sought publicity by damaging buildings considered bastions of male privilege. The Nevill Cricket Pavilion at Tunbridge Wells was one such, and in April 1913 it was completely destroyed after an arson attack.

In the summer of 1991, a phantom 12th man looted 10 cricket clubs in under two months, including seven in one afternoon. The thief, dressed in whites, helped himself to valuables from the fielding team's dressing-room. The raids were in Lincolnshire, Cambridge-shire and Bedfordshire.

Mrs Goodson's shop at the end of a row of cottages known as Farmer's Terrace in Bath had a plate-glass window about eight feet long by six feet high. It became a popular target for the batsmen of the local cricket club, who regularly 'holed out', much to the lady's rage. As yet another cricket ball smashed through the window, she would appear at her shop door in old cloth cap and white apron shaking her fists and shouting abuse at all within earshot.

DISPENSATION

Sidmouth were batting and the ball was hit down towards the esplanade. A visiting fielder chased after it at full-pelt and, on reaching the edge of the ground, leapt over the wall in the belief that the beach lay immediately on the other side. A stunned silence engulfed everyone as he disappeared from view, plunging on to the road below. Luckily, he was only slightly injured. Some eye-

Geronimooo!

witnesses swear he yelled 'Geronimo!' as he jumped.

Thomas Barker was travelling with the Nottinghamshire team to play Hampshire at Southampton in 1843, when he was thrown out of the horse-drawn cab in London and broke his leg. The accident virtually finished his career.

A polio outbreak led a British Railways team from Carlisle to refuse to play a Junior Cup Final in Workington in 1956. The venue was changed to Keswick.

Thomas Sinclair of the North-West Fur Trading Company in Canada showed his appreciation of pioneering local cricket by 'giving the teams a gallon of sherry, procured and drunk upon the field'. As the old gentleman was leaving the scene of action, he nearly had reason to regret his liberality. A ball struck with tremendous vigour by an inebriated cricketer 'passed so swiftly and so close to his spectacles that he did not see it until a taller friend standing close beside him dropped to the ground with horrible groans and discoloured face, having received the missile in the ribs'.

In May 1901, six-year-old Leonard Baldwin was sitting with his aunt, Mrs Holder, on Malden Wanderers' cricket ground watching a game, 'when a gust of wind blew over one of the large sightscreens. The

structure knocked the lad over and fractured his left thigh . . .' He was cared for by Dr Davison, who at the time was President of the club.

A Mr Bowran bloodied his face against the fence in a great effort to pull off a catch. On being helped from the field, he was asked whether he wanted a doctor or dentist or a vicar – all of whom were in the side.

'None of them,' he gasped, 'I just want my bank manager' (also in the side).

Imran Khan, helping to spearhead Unicef campaigns, was brought to a realisation of the suffering of many by a visit to a hospital in Pakistan to see a young boy whom he had accidentally hit on the head with a cricket ball.

Twelve-year-old Hugh Carling, whose ambition was to play for England, was not deterred by shrapnel wounds suffered in an IRA bomb blast at Victoria Station. Six weeks later, he was being coached by former England batsman Clive Radley in a three-day MCC School course at Lord's.

DESPATCH

In 1737, John Boots died while playing cricket at Newick in Sussex, after colliding with George Wall when both were running across the wicket. What would a contemporary tabloid newspaper have made of it? 'Boots kicks bucket after collision with wall', perhaps?

The Revd Harry Williams turned out for Wytham on the Hill in Lincolnshire in 1834. He was vicar of Mauldon and perpetual curate of Cheseldon, both in Surrey, and was staying for a three-week holiday with his brother-in-law Major-General Johnson. Wytham were short in numbers for a local game and so the Reverend was co-opted into the team. After a spell of bowling, he walked a few yards away from the wicket, 'fell flat on his face and on being picked up was found to be quite dead'. The coroner returned a verdict of death through apoplexy.

Julius Caesar, a temperamental yet highly rated upper-order batsman who went on the first tours to North America and Australia, killed a gamekeeper during a shooting party when his gun went off accidentally. Poor Caesar never really recovered from the shock and his health went into decline.

Richard Boys, who played one match for Lancashire in 1877, died when an industrial chimney fell on him at Burnley in 1896.

Richard Wardill, who scored the first century in Australian first-class cricket for Victoria against New South Wales at Melbourne on Boxing Day, 1867, committed

suicide by jumping into the Yarra River in 1873. He had embezzled £7000 while working as an accountant for the Victoria Sugar Company and the fraud had just been discovered.

A Middlesex player for one match only, John Boak also appeared for New South Wales and Queensland. He was killed by a train while crossing a railway line at Bermondsey in 1876.

Fred Bull, off-break bowler for Essex and one of *Wisden's* Five Cricketers of 1898, whom CB Fry saw as having 'all the requisites – a natural spin, a mastery of length, and a long repertoire of tricks', was in the end a victim of doubts about the legitimacy of his bowling action.

He drowned himself at St Anne's in 1910 with a 7lb stone tied around his neck. Bull thoughtfully had first returned his room-key to his landlady.

Gilbert Dawson, opening right-hand batsman for Hampshire between 1947 and 1949, was found dead in his crashed car in Glasgow in 1969.

William Jupp, cousin of the well-known Surrey opening batsman Henry Jupp, was killed by an accident on the cricket field at the age of 26. William, who had also played for Surrey on two occasions in first-class matches, but more often for Dorking, was taking part in a minor match at

Woking. High catches were being exchanged between the fall of wickets and Jupp was jostled just as he was about to catch the ball. He missed and it fractured his skull.

The Middlesex Chronicle of 28 June 1770 reported that a Mr Johnson, a goldsmith of London Wall, died from a blow he received from a cricket ball while playing near Islington.

The Middlesex Journal of 8 August 1772 recorded a lad playing in a match on Kennington Common who was struck by the ball while at the wicket and had the bridge of his nose broken. He died the following day.

Northants batsman William Davidson, a Scot from Kincardineshire, was killed in 1915 at Rouen, France. At the time, he was 65 years of age and thought to be the oldest first-class cricketer who perished in action during the First World War.

The Revd William (Manstead) Benton, who played in two matches for Middlesex at the age of 40 in 1913, was killed in action on the Somme in 1916.

The Revd William Bury, hard-hitting batsman for Cambridge University, Northants and Notts, twice experienced intimations of his own mortality when reading

premature obituary notices within a few months in 1920. It was a case of third time unlucky seven years later.

In the *Wisden Book of Cricketers' Lives*, Benny Green highlights the case of a cricketing funeral begetting a cricketing funeral. Arthur H Gregory, of the great Australian cricketing dynasty, fell off a tram when returning from the burial of his cousin SE Gregory, 'and was returned to the cemetery much sooner than he or anyone else could reasonably have expected'.

> *Cricket on pitches like ours bears the same relationship to true first-class cricket that target shooting bears to Russian roulette.*
> Malcolm Winter on Northants v West Indies, *Sunday Times*

Diminutive Johnny 'Boy' Briggs, one of the most popular professionals of his era, suffered from a particularly serious type of epilepsy which affected him during several important matches, notably the Headingley Test of 1899. Eventually, he was confined to Cheadle Asylum, where he died in January 1902 at the age of 39.

Wanstead's groundsman, Hockheimer, formerly a professional to Lord Sheffield in Sussex, umpired a match between the club and Essex Club and Ground in 1909. A slow leg-spinner, Dr Holton, who habitually ran across the wicket

'Ah, I feel better already, Dr Bourke!'

after delivery, was bowling when the batsman hit a fierce straight drive. The doctor dodged out of the way at the last moment and Hockheimer, whose sight-line had been obscured, was hit by the ball. He was taken to hospital and died several days later.

The Earl of Dalkeith, Eton and MCC upper-order batsman, accidentally shot himself while deer-stalking.

In 1881, the eighteen-year-old opening batsman Nathaniel Hone, who was about to play for Na Shuler – The Wanderers – against Limerick, met with a fatal accident.

Hone and other members of the team were staying at Cleary's hotel in Limerick just opposite a medical practitioner called Dr Bourke. On the morning of the match, Hone stepped across the road to obtain a draught of medicine which had been prepared the night before by one of Bourke's assistants. Through some dreadful mistake the potion contained a strong admixture of carbolic acid. Hone had barely crossed back to the hotel when he collapsed and then, later that day, passed away.

Charlie McGahey was an attacking batsman who captained Essex and played full-back in his time for Tottenham Hotspur, Arsenal and Sheffield United.

In a game against Oxford University he was bowled by Robertson-Glasgow, later of Somerset and a renowned writer.

In the pavilion McGahey was asked how he had been dismissed.

'Well,' said Charlie, 'a most extraordinary thing happened. I was bowled by a gentleman I thought had been dead hundreds of years – a fellow called Robinson Crusoe.'

'Crusoe', of course, became Robertson-Glasgow's *nom de plume*. Sadly, in a fit of depression, he took his own life. McGahey died of septic poisoning.

Opening batsman Charles Bull, Kent and Worcestershire, who scored 1000 runs in a season four times, was killed in a road accident at Margaretting in Essex in 1939.

Ken Davidson, middle-order right-hand batsman for Yorkshire and Scotland in the 1930s before emigrating to the USA where he excelled at badminton, was killed in a plane crash at Prestwick in 1954.

Jeffrey Stollmeyer, former West Indian opening batsman and selector, a highly regarded figure in Caribbean cricket, was savagely murdered by intruders to his property.

Ian Bedford, one-time Middlesex captain who led MCC tours to South and North America, and a lauded leg-spinner who failed to maintain his early promise, collapsed while batting in a club match at Buckhurst Hill in 1966 and died on the way to hospital.

In Sri Lanka, 18-year-old M Nilam died after being struck by a stump-wielding umpire and in India, Vasant Pimple, an umpire, died after being struck by a stump-wielding wicket-keeper.

CURIOSITIES

Some games are quaint and quirky. Some cricket is quirky and quaint . . .

Shipdham, beaten by Swaffham in 1769, put their defeat down to 'the superior skill of Masonry in their adversaries, many of the Swaffham side belonging to the Lodge in that town and other Lodges, and, of course, were better judges of Right Lines, Angles and Distances, with the only true method and secret hour to level a wicket, or cut the horizontal bale'.

A case of Masons lodging an appeal

'A controversial selection, obviously . . .'

In a one-day game in Pakistan involving the Nazimabad Sports side and Clifton Gymkhana, four motorcyclists roared on to the pitch from different directions, seized the Clifton captain, Test cricketer Aftab Baloch, and forcibly shaved off his hair. As the assailants carried knives, none of the other players dared intervene. Apparently, Aftab had been chosen as a victim because he had dropped a player from the team. The player had taken his revenge by calling in the 'heavies'.

The Gentlemen of Kent played the Gentlemen of England at Canterbury in 1842. There were *159* extras in the match.

Play was stopped at Curdridge, near Southampton, when a hot-air balloon advertising a new burger restaurant ran out of fuel sooner than expected and was brought down to land neatly between the stumps during a match in 1982 between Curdridge and Medstead.

At Marnhull, Dorset, a batsman was set alight when a box of matches in his pocket ignited after being struck by a ball. He retired rapidly to square-leg to seek the partial concealment of the umpire's billowing coat, where he removed his trousers amid much smoke and confusion.

Included in a History of Kendal Cricket Club, there appears this 'graphic' description:
First XI v Next 16 at Kendal, 1861, August 10: 'Troughton hit the "leather" about carelessly for 44, Savage daringly for 21, Burnett indifferently for 23, Dunsdale determinedly for 13, Hargreaves stiffly for 13, T Calderwood scientifically for 11; a brace of sixes, with extras, complete the 163.'

The *London Chronicle* for 1761 (Tuesday, 21 April, to Thursday, 23 April):
On Monday afternoon a great match at a fingle-hand Cricket was played on Epfom Downs for 100 guineas, between the famous Baker of Ewell and a young fellow, known by the name of Die Game, of Headly; the Baker went in firft and got 65 notches, on which the bets ran high againft Die Game, but he beat his antagonift after a conteft of upwards of four hours. A large fum of money was won and loft on this match.

In late January 1879, two cricket teams from Keswick played on skates on the frozen Derwentwater Lake.

Lord Winchilsea introduced an experiment in 1797 whereby four stumps were used instead of three and the wickets were two inches higher. 'By this alteration the game is rendered much shorter, by being frequently bowled out.' The move failed to gain general acceptance.

One of the longest adjournments ever known in a game of cricket was at Stoke Down in Hampshire. A match commenced on 23 July of one year and, after three days' play, was recommenced on 28 June of the next year.

At Shillinglee Park in 1843, the Earl of Winterton's XI beat *37* labourers by five wickets. Three years later, the same eleven were matched against *56* labourers. This time the game was not completed.

In a match played at Ticehurst in 1825, a hit from Thomas Cooper was caught on the point of a knife which was being used by a woman named Stapley; she kept a gingerbread stall on the ground. Her hand was badly cut by her involuntary action and the ball was so deeply perforated that considerable force was needed to withdraw the knife.

Music teacher and church organist Charles Hodsoll was playing against Camberwell when a ball ran up the handle of his bat and disappeared. He immediately shook himself, thinking the ball had come to rest in the folds of his jacket, or between jacket and shirt. However, no amount of rhythmic movement could produce a ball.

Just as the wicket-keeper stepped up to join the search, Hodsoll realised the ball had somehow nestled in his pocket. The wicket-keeper then tried to grab it and Hodsoll, fearing he would be given out, started to run round the field. With several fielders and the stumper in hot pursuit, the batsman managed by

You'll never catch me . . .

*Anderson's cure
for insomnia*

shirt and thence into his trousers. The *Penrith Herald* reported in detail:
'If he took the ball out he was out for touching the ball while in play; if he stood where he was till a fielder removed it before it touched the ground, he was caught out. After a moment's pause he ran for it, attempting to get out of the boundary and then take the ball out. Pursued by the eleven, he made a circuit of half the ground and was eventually pulled down inside the flags, and in the mêlée which ensued the ball was shaken clear, and the umpires decided Platt was not out.'

> 'He looks and bats like a librarian: a prodder and nudger with a virile bottom hand that works the ball to the on side and a top hand for keeping the other glove on.'
> Mike Selvey, *The Guardian*, on Bert Vance making his Test debut for New Zealand v England, Wellington, 1988

degrees to work the ball out of its pouch and on to the ground without touching it by hand. He also regained the crease before being run out.

A similar incident took place at Whitehaven in 1881, when in a match between the United England Eleven and Eighteen of the Town, a batsman called Platt hit a ball which lodged in his

George Anderson, a member of the All-England XI for 20 years and a proud professional to boot – he refused the captaincy of Yorkshire because it would mean having to play Surrey, with which club there had been considerable disharmony – occasionally had difficulty in getting to sleep. Whenever that happened he went downstairs, picked up his bat and took it to bed with him.

Gibb tucks in

Matches are frequently interrupted by rain, stray dogs or pieces of paper blowing across the pitch. On one occasion, however, in 1910, at Purton in Wiltshire, an aeroplane stopped play. Louis Bleriot, who in the previous year had become the first man to fly across the English Channel, landed on the village ground during a tour of England.

England, Yorkshire and Essex wicket-keeper Paul Gibb was renowned for his gargantuan appetite. After two lunch courses, it was not unknown for him to polish off an entire bowl of sherry trifle or fourteen pêche Melbas. One day, on a coastal steamer off Bombay, Joe Hardstaff of Notts wagered a substantial sum in rupees that Gibb could not eat 20 large slabs of ice-cream at one sitting. He managed it easily – in fact, he consumed 22 ices and then offered Hardstaff the chance of double or quits if he was allowed to continue on two massive tureens of fruit salad.

> 'I'm back now – and I intend to stay here as long as the mince pies hold out.'
> Ian Botham, after his four-wicket haul against the West Indies in 1991

On a Frogs CC tour of the Netherlands, a Dutch customs official who had apparently never seen cricket equipment, insisted on sawing a bat in half to ensure it was not hollowed out and containing contraband.

In a match against Bath in 1877, the Box captain tried twenty-one changes of bowling before capturing the first wicket with the score at 97.

'Er, when I said I had no intention of declaring . . .'

'Listen, he's brought the spinner on at this end'

A hole measuring 10ft x 12ft x 8ft deep appeared in the middle of Lindal Moor Cricket Club's ground in 1968 after a spate of wet weather: an old tunnel of iron ore workings had collapsed. Local folklore had it that in days long gone those below could tell who was bowling up above by the rhythmic pattern of their run-up.

During a soporific match between Sussex and Leicestershire, John Snow, who had a gift for doing the unexpected, decided to create a diversion.

The ball he bowled to Peter Marner was of smaller size than usual and consisted entirely of red soap. Marner's flashing blade smashed it into smithereens, whereupon everyone dissolved into helpless laughter. The scorebook tells but part of what happened: 'Ball exploded.'

Not many years ago, there was an optimistic advert in the personal column of *World Sport*. 'Refined Gentleman wishes to meet widow with two tickets for the Third Test; view to matrimony. Kindly send photograph of tickets.'

Players used to recover the ball from the River Eden alongside Appleby's cricket ground with a special net. On the far side of the river lies the churchyard and when a burial took place cricketers used to stand reverently, with heads uncovered, until the cortège left.

Charles Payne, playing against Hastings for Tunbridge Wells in 1863, hit to leg a ball from John Sands from which he scored 13 runs – 12 for the stroke and one for an overthrow. The ball ran away 'down the Common' from the chasing fielder on a sloping pathway.

Just before World War Two, there was an experiment in South Africa with what was called 'Midnight Cricket'. Visionary thinking resulted in the balls and stumps being covered with phosphorus paint. For a while the popularity of ghostly games in the gloaming led to talk of a night-time cricket league.

In Ceylon, as it was then called, a near-riot by spectators happened because, having been charged one rupee to sit on the branches of a tree overlooking the ground, they were expected to pay another rupee to be allowed to land and walk away.

At Penrith in 1879, cricketers and bowling club members were in opposition. They played each other at both games and added the scores together.

A huge petrol tank at Adelaide in South Australia was a venue for cricket. The tank was about 100 feet wide and built to hold two million gallons. The game was illuminated by electric light and runs were scored according to the actual place where the ball struck the side of the tank.

Because of a points anomaly in a game partly affected by rain, two Yorkshire League clubs, Batley and Gomersal, adopted role reversal in a strange game in 1979: Batley tried to lose their own wickets and Gomersal tried *not* to get them. The match became farcical when Batley's captain deliberately hit his own wicket, but was given not out because there had been no appeal by the fielding side.

LITERARY LINKS

It is noticeable how quickly on retirement some cricketers swop togs for typewriters – and not only on retirement. The reverse is equally true. How little persuasion is needed to make literary luminaries desert their blank sheets of paper in order to make similar blobs on cricket scorecards. Mind you, for WG Grace, who thought that reading and writing were bad for cricketers' eyesight, it was all Latin and Greek . . .

In Memorium Gloriosam Ludorum Etoniensium, Harroviensium, Wykehamicorumque, nuper intermissorum anno 1854
A Latin skit by Frederick Gale on the matches of the three public schools.

Homeric Games at an Ancient St Andrews, 1911
A short epic poem in Greek in part describing a *kriket* encounter between the Phosiloi (a team of male veterans) and the Amazones (pupils of a girls' school).

> *'He would win the toss, then retire to a hot bath, to perspire and exude last night's champagne.'*
> **Neville Cardus on the Honourable Lionel Tennyson**

Many writers have fantasised that William Shakespeare knew something about cricket due to the presence of such lines in his plays as:

'What work's, my countrymen, in hand? Where go you
With bats and clubs?'
Coriolanus, Act 1, Scene 1

'O, let the hours be short
Till fields, and blows, and groans applaud our sport'
Henry IV, Act 1, Scene 3

'We may outrun,
By violent swiftness, that which we run at,
And lose by overrunning'
Henry VIII, Act 1, Scene 1

'Stand! and go back. Back, I say, go; back – that is the utmost of your having, – back'
Coriolanus, Act 5, Scene 2

'Take heed, be wary how you place your [feet]'
Henry VI, Part 1, Act 3, Scene 2

'I had rather be set quick i' the earth
And bowled to death with turnips'
Merry Wives of Windsor, Act 3, Scene 4

'Take my cap – Jupiter!'
Coriolanus, Act 2, Scene 1

'And have is have however men do catch'
King John

'Such wanton wild and usual slips as are companions'
Hamlet

'How now, good Blunt, thy looks are full of speed'
Henry IV

'It strikes me past the power of comfort'
King John

'Yet would I know that stroke would prove the wicket'
Othello

'I would give a thousand pounds I could run as fast as thou canst'
Henry IV

'I'll strike nothing'
Two Gentlemen of Verona

'An honest man, look you . . . a marvellous good neighbour, faith and a very good bowler'

Love's Labour's Lost

'A hit, a very palpable hit!'

Hamlet, Act 5, Scene 2

'Beaten, but not without honour!
In this glorious and well-
    foughten field,
We kept together in our chivalry.
I shall have glory by this losing
    day,
So call the field to rest, and let's
    away
To part the glories of this happy
    day'

*Henry V, Act 4, Scene 2, and
Julius Caesar, Act 5, last scene*

O, that it were so. The Bard of Avon was probably far too busy on the South Bank to have even heard of John Derrick and his playing at cricket mentioned in the court hearing at Guildford, which took place in his lifetime.

By comparison, two and a half centuries later, another literary genius, Charles Dickens, knew and appreciated the game. Irving Rosenwater, in a monograph on *Charles Dickens and Cricket*, tells how George Dolby, the manager of his reading tours, said: 'Mr Dickens was a great lover of cricket, and in the summer of 1866 he would often hurry back to Gad's Hill after a visit to town, in order to be present at a cricket match in the field at the back of his house – between his own Higham Club and some other club in the neighbourhood.' Dickens was known to have spent a whole day 'notching a match' and he also arranged a number of charity games at Gad's Hill in which 'it was his habit to contribute a guinea if the first ball – the one normally bowled by him – was hit to the boundary'.

The All-Muggleton and Dingley Dell match and the single-wicket confrontation in the West Indies between Jingle and Sir Thomas Blazo from *Pickwick Papers* are the best-known examples of Dickens on cricket. There are many other passing allusions in his novels and writings, i.e.:

The Old Curiosity Shop (Chapter xxv)
Martin Chuzzlewit (Chapters iv and v)
Great Expectations (Chapter xxvii)
The Holly Branch (Second Branch)
A Flight
The Child's Story
A Christmas Tree
Bleak House (Chapter iv)
The Schoolboy's Story
Little Dorrit (Book II, Chapter vi)
The Mystery of Edwin Drood (Chapter xvii)
*Uncommercial Paper,
Dudborough Town
Sunday under Three Trees*

In this last brochure, Dickens makes it obvious that he sees no moral objection to cricket after church:

'I was surprised to hear the hum of voices and occasionally a shout of merriment from the meadow beyond the churchyard; which I found, when I reached the stile, to be occasioned by a very animated game of cricket, in which the boys and young men of the place were engaged, while the females and old people were scattered about: some seated on the grass watching the progress of the game, and others saunter-ing about in groups of two or three, gathering little nosegays of wild roses and hedge flowers.

'I was in the very height of the pleasure which the contempla-tion of this scene afforded me, when I saw the old clergyman making his way towards us. I trembled for an angry interrup-tion to the sport, and was almost on the point of crying out, to warn the cricketers of his approach; he was so close upon me, however, that I could do nothing but remain still, and anticipate the reproof that was preparing. What was my agreeable surprise to see the old gentleman standing at the stile, with his hands in his pockets, surveying the whole scene with evident satisfaction! And how dull I must have been, not to have known till my friend the grandfather (who, by-the-bye, said he had been a wonderful cricketer in his time) told me, that it was the clergyman himself who had established the whole thing: that it was his field they played in; and that it was he who had purchased stumps, bats, ball and all.'

George Henry Remnant, who played for Kent and once in minor cricket scored two double centuries in a match, was a friend of Dickens.

As a young man, Remnant was a member of the village side at Gad's Hill, Higham. He was fond of relating how, during a game in the meadow adjoining Dickens' house, he drove a ball into the back of a trap in which sat the novelist's children with their governess. The noisy arrival of the missile caused the pony to take fright and bolt. Remnant gallantly dropped his hat, dashed in pursuit and managed to pull up the runaway before any harm was done.

'Hambledon is a place that I have a strong dislike to, on account of its morals and dissipation.'
Revd Gilbert White in a letter to his brother, Revd John White, 1774

Little Tom Clement is visiting at Petersfield, where he plays

much at cricket: Tom bats, his grandmother bowls; and his great-grandmother watches out!
Revd Gilbert White
in a letter to his nephew

Charles Lamb joined in the booing on the first and last night of his comedy *Mr H* in order, perhaps, to remain unnoticed in the theatre. The leading character was called Hogsflesh 'after the famous cricketer of that name', who as a source of amusement was disappointing.

Thomas Beagley, Hampshire hitter, a bricklayer and carpenter with a robust, stooping frame and immense hands and feet. 'In figure and appearance compared to Samuel Johnson, the great lexicographer. There was nothing un-English about him barring a French wife.'

Some literary giants who have wielded a bat with exactly the right attitude if not entirely the right aptitude include JM Barrie, Sir Arthur Conan Doyle, Herbert Farjeon, Ian Hay, EW Hornung, Andrew Lang, EV Lucas, AG Macdonnell, George Meredith, AA Milne, John Moore, Siegfried Sassoon, Hugh de Selincourt, RC Sheriff, JC Snaith and JC Squire. Edmund Blunden would have denied that he was more adept at the crease than most of the above, but he was.

JM Barrie and A Conan Doyle, both left-arm spinners, sat on the beach at Aldeburgh in Suffolk throwing pebbles into the sea. They were engrossed in cobbling together the musical *Jane Annie*, in which the Proctor's song reflected their favourite recreation:

In an abstract way (though I don't
    care to play)
I think very deeply of cricket
And prove that because of dynamical
    laws
It's easy to keep up one's wicket
I could score without doubt my
    hundred not out,
Though modesty makes me refrain,
And the whiz of a ball is not
    soothing at all
To a man with a sensitive brain.

His MCC-ey
And WG-ey
Lord's-and-the-Ovally brain.

Barrie, an ardent devotee of cricket, was keeping wicket one day when a batsman noted for his pedantry arrived at the crease. 'If I strike the ball with even the slightest degree of impulse,' remarked the batsman, 'I shall immediately commence running with considerable velocity.'

Barrie, recalling the words later, added wryly: 'There was no occasion for him to commence.'

The poet Robert Graves played cricket during a lull in hostilities at the Battle of Vermelles in 1915. He and his fellow soldiers cut down a rafter to use as a bat and wrapped together some rifle rags to make a ball. The wicket was a birdcage containing the corpse of a parrot.

Fellow poet Siegfried Sassoon was an able cricketer who appeared many times for Blue Mantles and occasionally for Tunbridge Wells CC. He was too modest in his assessment of his ability: 'To be candid, the cricket was a good deal better than I was; but by being available if someone "chucked" I often obtained a place in the side at the eleventh hour.'

> *Henry Bates, whose general appearance resembled that of the character of Wilkin Plammack in Scott's* Tales of the Crusaders, *was tall and bulky and lived at Woolwich. 'In advancing to deliver the ball he was reminiscent of the moving towers used in ancient Rome warfare.'*

Sassoon's chilling reminder of the First World War in *The Dreamers*:

I see them in foul dug-outs,
gnawed by rats,
    And in the ruined trenches, lashed
by rain,
    Dreaming of things they did with
balls and bats.

'The bat is indescribable. A mass of willow, slightly rotten in places and resembling a mop at the bottom. The handle is said to be cane, but one player who has had a most extensive and varied acquaintance with canes, both at home and abroad, says that no cane *ever* stung like this bat, so it must be of some foreign substance. The balls go, some into the side windows of the school, some through those of the factory, others again attach themselves to the windows opposite.'

TE Lawrence on
'Playground Cricket'

I wish you'd speak to Mary, Nurse
She's really getting worse and worse,
Just now when Tommy gave her out

She cried and then began to pout
And then she tried to take the ball
Although she cannot bowl at all.
And now she's standing on the pitch
The miserable little Bitch!
          Hilaire Belloc,
          'The Game of Cricket'

AA Milne used to confound batsmen and wicket-keepers by delivering balls from behind and over the heads of umpires.

After a match between Beaconsfield and a team of Authors and Publishers captained by the ubiquitous JC Squire, a dinner was held during which a cricket ball was thrown around the room.

Eventually, it was caught by the renowned writer and poet, GK Chesterton, who immediately rose to his feet and said: 'It is with very special pleasure that I propose the health of this admirable ball, firstly because this ball and I share a common rotundity . . .'

The question of knowing celebrated cricketers personally is a difficult one. On the basis of a twelve-minute conversation with Mr Bailey, in 1960, at Romford, am I justified in referring to him as Trevor? This is a question which every individual must decide for himself. Let him look in his heart and ask. If I do this, I invariably find the answer is 'Yes'.

          Stephen Potter

'A curious cricketer who, after opting for the slips, dropped three catches and drank lemonade in the pavilion.'

          Malcolm Elwin

'The Colonel, like so many myopic cricketers, failed to observe that seagulls face the wind!'

          Malcolm Elwin

Arthur Conan Doyle, batting for MCC against Kent, was being given a torrid time by the pacey WM Bradley. One ball landed with a thud on the batsman's thigh. The pain suddenly became unbearable and Conan Doyle in a panic pulled out the scorching contents of his trouser pocket – a box of Vestas ignited by the impact – and threw them on the turf. WG Grace, who was fielding nearby, could not stop laughing and squeaked in his high voice: 'Couldn't get you out – had to set you on fire.'

Henry Winter's limerick competition in *The Independent* produced the following from a Doncaster doctor, John Felton:

A team that was packed full of Rambos
With the guile of 10 Oliver Tambos,
I'm sure you would see,
Would certainly be
Dismissed just as Curtly by Ambrose.

Another from Margaret Bower of Bigbury, Devon:

Ms R Heyhoe Flint said 'I see,
the MCC's all MCP,
So girls, don't be a martyr,
Be like Lysistrata,
And in the pavilion refuse to make tea.'

Incendiary, my dear Watson

From Francis Bailey of
Liverpool in *The Diary* jotted by
Neil Wilson:
   'Father, why's it called Lord's?'

'Because, son, it only accords
Privileged entry
To PM's and gentry
And bugger us plebeian hordes.'

THE GAME IS BUT A STAGE

Of all the Joys our Parents did Partake,
From Games Olympic, down to Country Wake;
To one more noble they cou'd ne'er refort
Than CRICKET! CRICKET! ever active Sport.

Part of an epilogue to a play 'defir'd by the Gentlemen Cricketers of Barrow' and spoken by one Geo. Alexander Stevens, who assumed the character of a cricketer. The lines appeared in *The Norwich Mercury* in September 1744, one of the first references in the press to cricket in East Anglia.

Mr GL Barrett, cricketer and manager of the Norwich Cricket Club until the side dispensed with his services after a dispute, played opposite the famous actress Mrs Siddons, at the Theatre Royal in the City in September 1788.

The *Accrington Times*, reporting on a game between Haslingdon and King and Casey's Clown Cricketers in 1873:

'The Clowns, in addition to their cricketing qualifications, possessed other means of entertaining the spectators. One named the Shakespearian Clown, performed very cleverly the trick of catching a ball on a bat. Any person on the field was allowed to give him a bat and send a ball to him at as great a distance as it could be thrown and in all cases the clown caught the ball on the bat and steadied it there. He also performed the trick of carrying two wickets on the end of a third. The clowns on the whole elicited much laughter by their witty utterances and jests.'

> *'Lawrence has cut down both run and pace. His approach now resembles the young motorcyclists in training on the car-park, slaloming between cones as they kept their balance and their seats under the watchful eye of neighbourhood police.*
> *'Lawrence, apparently, has been no-balling wide on the return crease and from Thursday watchers at Lord's may witness the extraordinary sight of a Test bowler doing a waltz-step in mid-approach. He may be nicknamed Syd after a bandleader, but this is ridiculous!'*
> Robin Marlar, *Sunday Times*

The London Clown Cricketers failed to turn up for a match with Lymington CC in 1878. A report at the time suggested that they had mistakenly 'gone to Leamington, in Warwickshire'.

'Jan's First and Last Cricket Match' was a Devonian dialect tale of two people who were, almost indivisibly, one: AJ Coles, the creator, and Jan Stewer, the creation. Performed in theatres and halls throughout the West Country, including one in the presence of Queen Mary 'who was much amused', it was, as Jan said, 'all the talk fer weeks ahead 'bout this-yer Cricket Match. Up to the Black 'Oss you cude'n yer nothing else – so they tells me.' The story was immortalised to the extent that some Devon cricket teams still call the sightscreen the 'rin-jan'. At one point, when Jan and the parson are batting, Jan, on hearing the man of the cloth shouting at him to run, runs as fast as he can after the ball.

Actor John Brockbank, a Cumbrian-born batsman for Brecon, Cambridgeshire, Cumberland, Hereford, Shropshire, Staffordshire and MCC also found time to play soccer for England.

In 1904, entertainer George Robey opened the innings for Cardiff in a game against Swansea. He totalled 23 in his two innings.

Charlie Chaplin, whose cricketing heroes were Tom Hayward and Bobby Abel, never forgot the time when, as a young actor on tour in Nottingham, he paid half-a-crown for a stand seat to watch Surrey playing Notting-hamshire at Trent Bridge and it poured down. Years later, dining with cricket correspondent EW Swanton in Jamaica, Chaplin asked: 'Have you got around yet to giving a rain-check?'

Oliver Battcock, who appeared on stage as Oliver Gordon, and performed mainly at the Theatre

Royal Windsor and the Salisbury Playhouse, was a left-arm medium pace bowler who played for Harrow, MCC and Bucking-hamshire. He was reputed to have taken around 6000 wickets in non-first-class cricket.

Lord Olivier, perhaps forgetting the time when he had been cajoled, nay press-ganged, into playing for the Hollywood Cricket Club by Sir Charles Aubrey Smith, once said: 'I have often thought how much better a life I would have had, what a better man I would have been, how much healthier an existence I would have led, if I had been a cricketer instead of an actor.'

'When in the middle of a good innings my batting partner hit an early catch towards me, the desire for laughs overcame all other instincts. I dropped my bat and caught the ball. Such a bold defiance of the sport had its desired effect on the umpire. He ordered me off the field. Later, I was called to his room for six of the best. I didn't mind. I had won the round.'
John Le Mesurier on his schooldays, 'A Jobbing Actor'

Trevor Nunn, as a young director in the Royal Shakespeare Company, felt that his best friend in the company was the Aldwych stage door-keeper, Cliff. Cricket was a mutual love and one day Nunn was invited into the back-stage cubby-hole to watch the Test Match on an old black and white television set.

'England were playing the West Indies,' Nunn recalled, 'and

significantly failing to hold it together. I was aware there was another figure in the room and, every time an English wicket fell, out of the pitchy darkness came a voice that said things like "Oh, damn", or worse. I just assumed it was a quite junior member of the company. Then it was stumps and at 6.30 this figure got up and it was a lady wearing a brown suit. It still didn't click who it was and only after she had gone did I realise I had spent half-an-hour in this tiny little cubicle with Dame Peggy Ashcroft.'

'Peggy Ashcroft' – A biography by Michael Billington

Peggy Ashcroft had a passion for cricket. 'Harry Andrews remembers captaining a side against a women's team led by Peggy. The gentlemen batted left-handed and bowled underarm and the pre-arranged plan was that scores would finish level. The highly competitive Robert Shaw . . . would have none of this and swiped endless sixes. But, in the end, the Ian Botham of English acting was caught in the deep by Angela Baddeley. "I didn't," said Harry Andrews laconically, "put Bob Shaw on to bowl."'

'Peggy Ashcroft', Michael Billington

'Cricket is first and foremost a dramatic spectacle. It belongs with the theatre, ballet, opera and the dance.'

CLR James

It is 'the most frightening and entertaining game in the world. Talk about chess? Cricket is the sport of thinking gladiators.'

Norman Beaton, 'Beaton but Unbowed'

'Working with David is like being directed by a nice cricketer.'

Judi Dench talking about David Hare

'You can treat the white-clad players as performers in an obscure open-air ballet. For backdrop, there is the waving green of surrounding elms; for music, the smart crack of willow bat against leather ball.'

JA Maxtone Graham

'They've started this filthy floodlit cricket with cricketers wearing tin hats and advertisements for contraceptives on their boots.'

Toby in Alan Ayckbourn's 'A Gardener in Love, Intimate Exchanges'

'Among the equipment considered essential at most cricket matches, to the regret of most of the players some of the time and some of the players all of the time, there is a gentleman who is known, among many more colourful titles, as an umpire.'

Cardew Robinson

Robin Williams, the elastic-faced American comic actor, got the royal grin when he opined to Prince Charles: 'Cricket is basically baseball on valium'.

Sunday Times

'Skills learned on the cricket field will prove useful to Yorkshire-born actress Helen Baxendale,

Leg-breaks on the boards

who is preparing to bowl over
audiences in the Compass
Theatre's touring production of
Peter Shaffer's award-winning
play *Amadeus*.' So wrote the *Daily
Mail* Diary of 21-year-old
medium-pace bowler Helen, who

was Toyah Wilcox's stand-in for
the role of Mozart's wife,
Constanza. 'If I get bored I shall
practise my bowling action in the
dressing-room mirror,' said Ms
Baxendale, setting the pace for
Mozart.

NOTES TO PITCH
AND A
PITCH TO PLAY

Many people in the public eye relax at, or with, a game of cricket. Musicians, entertainers, celebrities, television pundits – no category is immune to its allure. An eclectic team choice might be: Julian Bream, the guitarist, who is quoted as saying: 'When my spinning finger is really working, I could turn them on a dung heap'; Patrick Moore, on record with: 'If I happen to connect with the ball it may go in any of 180 degrees or possibly into orbit'; cunning off-spinner Lord Lichfield; boxer John Conteh 'who can resist the temptation to spar outside the off-stump'; Tim Rice who runs his own Heartaches XI; Mick Jagger, who has played on many a foreign field; Peter Jay, who has played for Private Eye – and at cricket; John Alderton; Robert Powell; William Rushton, Uncle Bill Tidy and all . . .

'When I was watching Fred Astaire I used to think, here was a chap who would have been a great batsman.'

Sir Len Hutton

'When I was a little lad, I wanted to play cricket for Yorkshire and football for Huddersfield.'

Roy Castle

It is possible that the nine year-old Wolfgang Amadeus Mozart, composer *extraordinaire*, was introduced to cricket when staying, with his family, at the home of Sir Horatio Mann near Canterbury in 1765. Horatio, sole

surviving son of Galfredus Mann, was a fanatical patron of the game, a player himself in his days at Charterhouse and afterwards with Kent, and known in his time as 'The King of Cricket'.

AJD Edwards, secretary of London Schools Cricket Association, remarked on a resemblance between Graham Gooch and the composer Edward Elgar as he was c. 1903. Michael Kennedy, in the press, responded with: 'I suppose he has a point, though Elgar would have had a fit at the thought of "designer stubble". Sometimes, even today, Gooch's batting presents something of an enigma variation, but, on the whole, it has a majestic pomp and circumstance which is certainly Elgarian.'

Baritone Roy Henderson, who was 92 in 1991, was invited by Sir John Christie to sing the role of the Count in the first Glyndebourne production of *The Marriage of Figaro* in 1934.

When Henderson arrived he found that the musical director, Fritz Busch, doubting Christie's judgement, had sent his assistant to vet the singers. After he had listened to Henderson singing the Count's Aria, he turned to Christie and said: 'Good voice, but can he act?' Christie exploded. 'Of course he can act. The man's a cricketer!'

'I like music but cornet was out of tune, and they were playing Gilbert and Sullivan, and I was humming "Regular Royal Queen" to myself, and trying, at the same time, to watch out for Warwick Armstrong's top-spinner, and cornet kept worrying me all the time . . .'

George Gunn after scoring a Test century with an accompaniment provided by the Sydney Brass Band

Distinguished conductor, Sir Charles Groves, wrote: 'Cricket has been one of the passions of my life since I was introduced to it as a small chorister of St Paul's Cathedral. We had an asphalt playground on the roof of the Choir School, enclosed in wire and on which were two cricket nets and a "cradle" for improving our catching.' The 'cradle' was a present for 'steadiness' during a German Zeppelin raid.

'Watching Clinton steal a match in which Hick and Botham are playing is like going to a Pavarotti concert and seeing him upstaged by Des O'Connor. He is inelegant: a shoveller, scooper, nudger and smearer for whom the V between mid-off and mid-on is an exclusion zone. But he knows how to pace an innings and keep things ticking.'

Mike Selvey,
Surrey v Worcestershire,
Benson & Hedges Cup,
The Guardian

Richard Gordon, of the famous 'Doctor' series, enjoys recounting how he no-balled David Frost during a game at Bickley Park CC. 'Which is more than anyone's ever been able to do on the telly,' laughs Gordon.

Michael Parkinson on explaining cricket to Yanks: 'An impossible task, not because they are dumb but because cricket is a state of mind and not a sport. As Fats Waller said of swing: "If you've gotta ask you don't have it".'

Sir Robert Mayer, founder of Youth and Music Concerts, on his 100th birthday said: 'I don't really understand why 100 is so important – I suppose it has something to do with cricket.'

Reggie Crawford, a member of the family of cricketing Crawfords, had his appearances as an all-rounder over a ten-year period for Leicestershire restricted by his concert engagements. Crawford was a distinguished singer.

Astronomer and xylophonist Patrick Moore recalled in *The Journal of the Cricket Society* his 'finest hour' when he, a self-admitted 'rabbit' coming in at number 11 with the score at 27 for 9, hit a spectacular but extremely chancy 63, which enabled his team to win the match. 'The final verdict was given later by the Vicar, as we retired to the pub – which overlooked the sea shore. The Reverend pointed to a sandbank some way out to sea. "Care to walk across to that?" he asked. "If anyone is capable of walking on water, it must be you!"'

'If as I fear, there is cricket in heaven, there will also, please God, be rain.'

Arthur Marshall

BEASTS, BATS
AND BALLS

Our four-legged and feathered friends and even those without any feet have often tried to reassert their inalienable rights. The consequences have occasionally been sad and sometimes droll . . .

A mouse that is crazy for cricket
Is commonly known as a bat
The umpire is really a vampire,
I bet you didn't known that.

Roger Woddis,
Island of the Children

At Linsted Park in Kent there was once a game on horseback between the Gentlemen of the Hill and the Gentlemen of the Dale for a guinea a man. Whether or not they used long-handled bats polo fashion is not recorded.

The Nettleton side in Wiltshire once drew a match because a hit for what would have been a certain boundary struck a cow that had strayed on to the field of play.

Drake, a water spaniel owned by Lord Charles Kerr, took part in a game with servant James Bridger against J Cock Esq. and Wm. Wetherall in August 1813. The match, for 50 guineas a side, was played at Holt Pound Cricketing Ground near Farnham in Surrey.

'The post assigned to Drake was that of catching the ball, the only way indeed in which he could be serviceable; but as he always caught it at the first bound, he was, perhaps, a more expert and efficient partner than many bipeds.'

In a match between Gloucestershire and Surrey, a seagull held up play for several minutes by flying up and down the pitch.

In a game in rustic surroundings, the batsmen and fielders stood transfixed as no less than 15 weasels marched in solemn procession across the pitch from one boundary to the other.

There is a report of a game in Westmorland, during which a player left his braces on a hedge. They provided tasty fodder for a bullock who had sauntered up unobserved.

On the outskirts of Nairobi in Kenya dangerous animals have been known to interfere with play. One instance was noted by the writer George Mell. Apparently, a former Secretary for India, LS Amery, was among the spectators when a fielder was treading rather warily in trying to retrieve a ball that had been hit into the undergrowth. It was fortunate that he had been so cautious, for he almost stumbled over a lion chewing the leather to shreds.

The fielder, hastily retreating, claimed 'lost ball', but the umpire, at a safer distance, disallowed the appeal on the grounds that he knew where it was. 'Courage, mon brave!'

In order to kill worms which infested the recreation ground in East London, South Africa, arsenate of arsenic was laid. A little can kill worms and enough can kill human beings.

Naturally, the ball was bound to pick up some poison during play and cricketers were warned that if they suffered injury never to suck the wound unless they sought terminal dismissal.

Rowley Edward Potter, one time Dartford cricketer and treasurer and descendant of the parish long stop of 1759, was killed by a runaway horse while walking on East Hill in 1876.

Hampshire's match against Middlesex in May 1865 was played at the Islington Cattle Market.

Cricket has many rituals, even by association. At Ebernoe in Sussex during the Horns Fair a sheep is roasted whole and the horns are cut off and presented to the top-scoring batsman.

Roberts, the Sussex professional, was bowling to Major Bentinck during a match at Alton in August 1921, and near the end of the flight of a ball a swallow got in the way and was killed instantaneously. The deviation in the direction of the ball took the Major by surprise and he was bowled. As he said ruefully afterwards: 'The decision takes some swallowing.'

John Farmer captaining Newick against Nutley in 1947 aped St Vitus when attacked by a swarm of flying ants. A team-mate remarked that 'he looked as if he was auditioning for a contemporary dance group'.

Charles Connery, slow bowler and even slower scorer, was just going in to bat at Budleigh Salterton when his captain Freddie Nunn rushed up to him and tucked a small shrivelled mammal, recovered from the rafters of the pavilion, into 'Con's pocket . . . 'Play with a dead bat, Con' – which he did.

> To me a fast bowler is like an animal. If he smells fear he will be after you twice as hard.
>
> Ian Chappell

In 1934, South Hampstead were fielding at Horsham when an enraged bull, which had escaped from the market, arrived on the scene. The square-leg umpire, realising that discretion was the better part of valour, sought the comparative safety of the pavilion. His colleague behind the stumps stayed at his post displaying considerable *sang-froid*, only because he fondly imagined that the animal was a female of the species.

'Old George' Youens, bowler for Uxbridge, owned a liver-coloured setter of whom he was fond. At one match on the Common, the dog became over-excited and persistently crossed and re-crossed the playing area. The bowler, whose over was being interrupted, angrily called out: 'George, if that dog crosses again I'll throw the ball at him'. 'All right,' replied George, trying to keep the peace, 'but don't kill him.' Almost immediately the dog ran across the pitch again,

'Right-arm over, is it?'

Fishing for the ball outside off stump?

the bowler threw the ball, hit the dog and it dropped dead.

An unfortunate grayling, swimming along the River Yorke one afternoon in 1934, decided to rise above water and was instantly struck and killed by a cricket ball that had been hit into the river by S Rayne in a game between Hawes and Aysgarth. A fielder retrieved both ball and fish which measured 10½ inches.

The honorary secretary of the East Molesey club, Mr Welbourn, gave a polite ultimatum to the opposition's captain. He had no alternative but to remove Mr Heniker-Gottley from the attack, even though it was to the detriment of the Molesey batsmen, because he was being hit so frequently into the River Thames that the club's aquatic fielder, a water spaniel, had refused to recover further balls.

In a game between Members of Parliament and the Press at Adelaide Oval the air was so thick with locusts that spectators lost sight of any cricket.

In 1837, W Rose of Lowther Newtown, Cumberland, with 'Neptune', his Newfoundland dog – which he had been training all summer – beat two of the Askham Cricket Club at single wicket.

In a county match at Worcester in 1899 a startled rabbit scuttled on to the pitch and ran in all directions at once. Play was held up for a short time only to be further interrupted a little later when the umpire was distracted by the antics of a pig.

David Heygate, fielding for Kettering, was joined by what seemed to be a friendly *sciurus carolinensis* – grey squirrel. When he attempted to make a fuss of the rodent, he was savaged for his pains.

In a game at The Hague between South Holland and Frogs CC, the gigantic Jongbloed-Unterhorst who scaled 20 stones and was over two metres tall, hit a towering six which 'unluckily descended on an unobservant hen, scratching for grubs on the boundary, landing in its right side and despatching it promptly to the paradise of poultry'.

It was said of Fred Morley, the Nottinghamshire cricketer of the late 19th century, that so bad a batsman was he that, as he came out on to the pitch at number eleven, the Trent Bridge horse would automatically take its place between the shafts of the roller.

'Cricket began when the first man-monkey, instead of catching a cocoa-nut thrown him playfully by a fellow anthropoid, hit it away from him with a stick which he chanced to be holding in his hand.'

HG Hutchinson

A HOICK AND A TONK

Nowadays the village team is just as likely to have the stockbroker, advertising johnnie and commercial traveller in its midst as the blacksmith, sexton and farm labourer. And the last three could just as easily be leaning against their parked Porsches with Pimms' in hand. Sophistication has struck. Perhaps it was always there . . .

Having, the other day, once again spent an afternoon in watching a village cricket match, I am again perplexed by the passion for that game which is displayed by those who cannot shine at it. They cannot bat, they cannot bowl, they leave their place on the field, they miss catches, they fumble returns: and yet every Saturday, there they are, often in perfect flannels, ready to fail once more.

EV Lucas

On July 25, 1803, Binfield beat Wargrave away. On the day of the return match it rained so heavily that Wargrave on arrival said they could not think of playing. Consequently, several Binfield players departed. Whereupon Wargrave said they would now play, went to the ground and 'called the game'. 'On their return home they obtained the two half-guineas deposit money from the stakeholder at the halfway house' – previously he had said he would not part with any money till both parties were in agreement – 'and spent Binfield's half-guinea.'

A Ringwood newspaper of 1850 reported: 'Female Cricketers. Eleven women of Lyndhurst and Minstead played other eleven of Poulner and Picket Post on Thursday, when the latter were victorious. *The scene was a disgusting one and altogether discreditable to the district.*'

In a match between Warmsworth and Barnby Dun in 1860, the last man for the latter side went in to bat in the second innings with a malt shovel. This was shattered after five balls and having, of necessity, to revert to an orthodox bat, he was bowled next ball.

One of the rules agreed upon at the founding of the Box Cricket Club at the Chequers Inn in 1870, was that 'all improper language be strictly avoided and that a fine of 3d. on each occasion be inflicted for improper language or smoking during the playing of matches'.

In the 1878 accounts of the Box Cricket Club there appears the following entry:
Charlotte (bringing Cricket Balls from Corsham) 3d.

Donald Bradfield, historian of the club, writes: 'Make of this what you will, the thought of a little girl carrying cricket balls in her pinafore all the way from Corsham to Box and being given three pennies for her trouble is not without a certain charm.'

> 'To go to a cricket match for nothing but cricket is as though a man were to go into an inn for nothing but drink.'
> Neville Cardus

There are a number of graves near the 'Tins' corner of Lymington cricket ground. A town inhabitant in his Will expressed the wish that his 'grave should be so placed that boys might stand on the stone to watch the cricket'.

The Minute Book of Cogenhoe kept by one Bill Lines describes typical village cricket club happenings in a laconic way:

18.8.23. White Melville Reserves. Cog. 130 WM 127: 'WM 91–3 so last man in went for tea and did not bat but last man to bat was not seen as a fielder. Umpires rowing.'

15.6.20. Little Houghton. Cog. 24 all out including 9 byes: 'Notton and Wager (6–10) had got 8 men out before the score was passed, chiefly through Riff sneaking short ones.'

14.8.20. Brafield: 'Lost for first time on record by 39 . . . to 49 . . . Of course the rugged pitch and the setting sun coming behind the bowler's arm just as our innings started were blamed.'

10.6.22. 2nd XI v Brafield: Cog. 19 – 'Brafield Juniors had taken advantage of the fact that our scorer was short-sighted and allowed him to miss about 6 runs,

but we finished them off for 18 much to our satisfaction.'

28.5.21. 'The annual fixture at Horton was revived and we found their umpire in good form and lost by 44 to 58.'

2nd team vs. Billing (A) a close game – Billing 42, Cog. 41, 'our last pair W Rainbow and K Warner, being separated by the 8th ball of the over owing to our umpire Solomon Jun. Having dropped his beans through excitement'.

The writer Hugh de Selincourt, who immortalised Storrington as Tillingfold in his cricket novels, once took the first nine wickets for the village in the days when they played with stumps painted pure white.

All the side were determined he should take the tenth. Cecil Waller deliberately sent down a widish delivery on the leg side from which the batsman got an edge and began to run. The worst fielder in the side at fine leg, who had often unkindly been told that he could use a white stick let alone stumps, hurled the ball in and scored a direct hit. The batsman was run out by yards. 'The best laid schemes . . .'

In 1961, Storrington were playing an all-day away game. Starting at 11.30 a.m. and finishing at 7.30 p.m. with 1½ hours allowed for lunch and tea, the captain decided that having had to face a new ball – only one ball per match – it would not be safe to declare before 4 p.m.

The seventh wicket fell at 3.50 p.m. with the score 316 for 7. The next two batsmen, Davis and Funnell, refused to go in and therefore Storrington were forced to declare. It must be one of the

She had a good innings . . .

few cases of recorded mutiny in the annals of cricket.

As it happened, the opposition were bowled out for 118 with twenty minutes to spare.

The funeral cortège was passing through the village. On the top of the coffin was a cricket bag. A bystander turned to his companion and said: 'My! He must have been a *keen* cricketer.' 'You mean he *is*,' said the companion, 'it's his wife's funeral – that's him walking behind – he's playing at half-past two!'

In 1971, the Hempstead side in Kent scored 250 for eight. They then skittled out their opponents, Stoke, for a paltry 5. Fourteen year-old Richard Dunn took 8 for 4, which caused his 'keeper' to rub bruised hands and say that 'it was the fastest bowling I've ever seen in village cricket'.

The village of Coldharbour near Dorking in Surrey honoured carpenter Reg Comber's fiftieth year playing for their team in an unusual way. They hired Kennington Oval for a day at a cost of £3000 plus VAT for a match between teams selected by the captain and the chairman. Comber at 62 was flabbergasted. 'I never thought I'd go there to play,' he said. 'I just hope my knees hold out.'

After Nostell St Oswald's had clinched victory against Treeton Welfare in the 1991 National Village Championship, their two Pakistani players, who had performed extremely well, were found to be ineligible. Nostell were disqualified and Treeton went on to the third round.

Kevin Iles, captaining Goatacre to their second victory in the National Village Championship final at Lord's in 1991, scored a century in 45 minutes. From the first 39 balls received he hit seven sixes and six fours.

CRICKETING CHESTNUTS

The club dinner. The cricket meet. The stories everyone has heard before and wants to hear again . . .

The ubiquitous WG was dashing off to the station one morning when a woman rushed up to him and said, breathlessly, 'Oh, Doctor, thank goodness I've got you. Can you come quickly. I think my twins have got the measles.' Replied Grace: 'I'm sorry, ma'am. I'm just on my way to Gloucester to play cricket and can't stop. But please contact me at the ground if their temperatures reach 210 for two.'

In the days when country house cricket was in vogue, members of the touring team were often invited to stay for the weekend. At a Saturday night ball following a day in the field, the famous Australian leg-spinner Arthur Mailey was asked by his aristocratic hostess if he would like to dance.
'No thank you, ma'am, I am a little stiff from bowling.'
'Oh rahlly,' she replied, 'so that is where you come from.'

Alec Skelding, Leicestershire bowler and later umpire, had a technique for diffusing tension when a close run-out decision was called for. He would say: 'Gentlemen, it's a photo-finish. But as I have neither the time nor the equipment, the batsman is not out.'

After he retired from playing, Skelding acted for a time as scorer for his county. One day, there was a difference of opinion in the scorebox over the total at close of play. A large crowd assembled outside the box, demanding the correct score. As the tumult grew louder and the prospect of a settlement seemed no closer, Skelding stuck his head out and beckoned to a small boy in the crowd. As he pressed a penny into the boy's hand, he said: 'Go and buy an evening paper. We'll get it from that.'

As told by the inimitable Brain Johnston:

'During Len Hutton's tour of Australia, Frank Tyson's tremendous speed caused dismay and destruction among batsmen wherever he bowled. On one occasion, when he was at his fastest, he had run through a side until it was the turn of the number 11 batsman to come in. Looking pale and apprehensive, he came down the pavilion steps, but was so nervous that he couldn't close the catch of the pavilion gate. A voice from the crowd shouted: "Leave it open, you won't be long!"'

Patsy Hendren was fond of telling this apocryphal tale. Once when travelling in a train on his way to a match he sat opposite an ashen-faced stranger, who had his coat collar turned up around his ears. He looked so unwell that

Patsy was moved to ask what was the matter. In a hoarse voice – barely audible – the man confided that he was a keen cricketer who had recently let down his side very badly by collecting five ducks in a row. Said sympathetic Patsy: 'Oh dear, oh dear, if ever I made five ducks in a row, I would cut my throat.' The stranger, hardly able to whisper, gasped, 'I have.'

'There was a slight interruption there for athletics.'
   Richie Benaud, referring to a
   Lord's streaker, BBC TV

'They had one at Twickenham, I remember, but I reckon ours was better.'
   Lt-Col John Stephenson,
   MCC Secretary

David Lemmon, in his biography of Essex captain Johnny Douglas, tells of an occasion when a bowling change took place when the opposing batsmen were on top:
'The skipper himself was bowling with his usual resolution, beating the bat and cursing and swearing at his misfortune that he was not collecting a wicket every ball, but at the other end there was a need for containment. He told Hubert Ashton that he was going to give Claude a few overs. Claude Ashton had bowled at University, but he was not a regular bowler. Nevertheless, he was given the task of closing up the other end. He bowled at a medium pace which the batsmen seemed to relish and runs came freely. Douglas continued to leap in excitement and swear in frustration at his own luck, and Hubert Ashton anticipated that Claude would be withdrawn from the attack after four or five

rather expensive overs, but no change was made.
   After an hour, with the position worsening, Hubert Ashton gathered courage to approach the skipper and suggest that the younger Ashton might be removed from the attack. "*******," said Douglas, "is he still bowling?" '

He was engaged and took his sweetheart around everywhere. His batting was poor and invariably he made a duck, but the moment he returned to her among the spectators he was ready with his excuses.
   At one match the first ball spreadeagled his stumps, and his lady friend watched him silently as he resumed his seat next to her.
   'Was the light all right, Harold?'
   'Oh, yes.'
   'And the wicket good?'
   'Couldn't be better.'
   'Was it a good ball to hit?'
   'Excellent.'
   'Then why were you out?'
   'Because, sweetheart, I couldn't bear the thought of you sitting here all alone without me at your side.'

As told by John Arlott:
'The incoming batsman was resplendent in completely new gear and he bore a bat unblemished by ball marks. He took guard somewhat negligently, imperiously ordered the sightscreen to be moved – and then moved back to its original position – before he settled to a stance apparently loosely adapted from that of WG Grace. The first ball slipped from the laughing bowler's hand and bounced gently down the leg side untouched by any of the

batsman's several efforts to hit it. The next was a full toss which he attempted to cut and missed; the next, a half-volley, at which he aimed the same stroke some seconds after his middle stump had gone down. For the first time he looked round the field, in valediction rather than enquiry, sighed and departed. As he did so, first slip turned to the wicket-keeper and asked: "How do you suppose he knows he's right-handed?"'

'I'm very sorry to hear that you think of retiring, George,' said the clergyman persuasively. 'You're still one of the best bats in the team, and we shall miss you badly if you drop out.'

'Aye, no doubt, sir,' said the villager dolefully. 'Goodness knows Ah don't want to stop playin'; me heart and soul's in the game, but me liver's dead agin' it.'

Silas 'The Finger' Squeeres, a Beckenham umpire, once gave a local captain out for a duck caught behind. Apparently, the appeal was loud enough to be heard by a man working on Penge gasworks. Silas extended his famous finger imperiously to the heavens, his eyes resting on a point in the sky behind the keeper. 'That was out, sir,' he said in a fruity voice to the departing victim.

'Look here,' was the angry riposte, 'my friends have come here to see me perform with the bat, not you pointing your finger, you – !' (Shades of Grace) And with that and more effectively his bat, he struck 'The Finger' on another part of his anatomy and would have done so again had not the fielders intervened.

In a match against Gloucester-shire, Yorkshire captain Brian Close was fielding in his usual position at forward short leg. The Gloucester batsman Martin Young received a short ball from Freddie Trueman which he hit straight onto the side of Close's head, from where it rebounded to first slip, who took the catch. The resolute Close seemed totally unperturbed. At the lunch interval, a concerned member remarked to him: 'That was a nasty blow. Why do you stand so close? (*unintentional*) What would have happend if the ball had hit you right between the eyes?' 'He'd have been caught at cover!' replied the fearless Close.

A cricket enthusiast, having watched his team get badly defeated, stopped the umpire as he was leaving the field.

'Where's your dog?' he demanded.

'Dog?' exclaimed the astonished umpire. 'What are you talking about?'

'Well,' explained the exasperated enthusiast, 'you're the first blind man I've met without one!'

RHYMES OF THE TIME

LOCK AND LAKER

Lock and Laker, the man-eating
pair,
They have no mercy Batsmen
Beware
Between them they harass and
vanquish the 'Foe'
and down come the wickets all in
a row
Oh, how they shine, these two
Surrey Stars
I'm sure that their Fame has
ascended to Mars
Maybe one day the Martian Race
Will come down to watch them
face to face
Lock and Laker, the man-eating
pair
They have no mercy Batsmen
Beware
Charlotte Field

> *The bat that you were kind
> enough to send,
> Seems (for as yet I have not tried
> it) good;
> And if there's anything on earth
> can mend
> My wretched play, it is that piece
> of wood.*
> **Cardinal Manning**

I KNEW YOU ONCE AND LOVE YOU STILL

I knew you once and love you
still
Dear cricket green beneath the
hill,
Enclasped by gently rising steeps
And chalky stream with peaty
deeps.
Dear cricket green beneath the
hill
I knew each blade and love you
still!
Watch pounding feet that gather
pace
And ball that swings with
swallow's grace –

Hear partner's call, when frantic
dive
Follows a cracking cover-drive
Or hissing slow from hooded
hand
The venomed balls and 'epic'
stand.

I knew you once and love you
still
Dear cricket green beneath the
hill,
And when the lengthening
shadows flow
And panic runs greet 'overthrow'
Strides jauntily the 'last man in'
A slogger he! and eight to win;
Soon lofted high o'er cowering
trees
Lost ball is sought on questing
knees.

I knew each blade and love you
still
Dear cricket green beneath the
hill

When dimming lights have left
the ground
And plaint of owl is only sound.
Yes, then oh then I love you still
In slumber sweet beneath the hill.

Bevan Whitney
(Poem from the museum at
Corfe, Dorset)

Cricket starts with the month of
May
Expenses starts the same,
But, the idle sods say what's the
odds?
So long as we gets a game.

I know the cost of loving is up
And beer is ninepence a tin,
That smokes are high and birds
are fly
And horses don't all come in.

But you finds the money for all of these,
And pays spot cash in the pub;
So, bowing low, I begs to know
Why the hell her don't pay yer sub?

FR Simon
Secretary/Treasurer
Nottingham Forest Amateur CC

LIMESTONE

Graham Mort

Poised under the sun's incineration
Men in white crane forward.

A dead silence.

Bowler treads his run-up,
Batsman takes stern guard
And waits to make a stroke.

Each summer the village team loan this field,
Mow the rough grass and mark a crease in lime;
Four stone walls mark the boundaries,
Beyond them hills spectate the ritual game.

Through the long afternoon
They bowl their spin and swing,
Are cut or driven away, until one ball
Turns in more sharply from the pitch
And a headstrong batsman swipes empty air –
Then a stump is taken clean out
And bails fly up towards the jubilant men.

First innings over
The beer tent is loud with talk –
Hay-time and cattle prices
And weather faired up –
As the players crowd in
To cram sandwiches and ale.

Above a stunted line of trees
The hills' white shoulders glare in sun,
Sculpted by ice and meltwater
Millions of years ago;
After a lifetime in the same valley
The men hardly spare them a glance now,
Their way of doing things
So ingrained with limestone.

Sun loses its stridency
And the game resumes.
Tree-shadows lengthen on stark slopes,
A skylark sings above mid-wicket,
Hanging as if carved from stone.

The ball soars to gruff cheers
And scuffs over a wall for six,
Scaring a lapwing from her eggs;
Hills gaze down,
Veiling with slow purple,
Waiting for and wanting nothing.

When the final ball is bowled
The keeper squats on his haunches,
Balanced for the take.
The bowler sends down a teasing leg-spinner
That curves in air an eternity
Before pitching to the bat;
The players cup their hands and wait,
Behind them the centuries' shadows lengthen.

From A Country on Fire

THE CRICKET CLUB OF RED NOSE FLAT

Jay Hickory Wood

Now, when a man identifies himself with certain acts,
It's very rude for any one to doubt that they are facts.
There are only two ways for it – you believe him, if you're wise;
If you're not, and he is little, then you tell him that 'he lies'.

So, as my friend was taller than myself by quite a head,
And a toughish-looking customer, I swallowed all he said.
But when at last he paused for breath, and also for a drink,
I thought I'd change the subject, so I said, 'No doubt you think
That cricket as a sport is very womanish and tame
Compared with scalping Indians. Do you understand the game?'

'Do I understand the game?' he said. 'Wall, stranger, you may bet
What I don't know 'bout cricket – wall, it ain't invented yet.
Perhaps you ain't aware, my friend, that 'way down Ole 'Frisco
We had a slap-up cricket club?' I said I didn't know.

'Wall, now you know,' he answered, 'and I'll tell you 'bout a game
We played there just a year ago as warn't so plaguy tame.'
And this is what he told me – of course it mayn't be true –
But as he told the tale to me I tell the tale to you:

'The boys 'way down in 'Frisco, though all a reckless lot, –
They'd most come out from England, – and had got a tender spot.
That spot it were the village green, where as boys they'd bowl and bat,
So we all made up our minds we'd have a club at Red Nose Flat.

We didn't have no captain – leastways we elected four,
But some one allus pistolled them, so we didn't vote no more.
You see, them captains allus tries to boss the blessed show,
Which ain't a healthy thing to do, 'way down in Ole 'Frisco.

Wall, we went ahead a-practising, as happy as could be,
Till Thunder Jack shot Blood-red Bill for hitting him for three.
And we held a general meeting, and we passed the following rule:
"A member pistolled on the field by members, in the cool,
Providing he is up to date in payment of his 'sub',
Is planted at the sole expense of this 'ere cricket club."
We heard as how a lot of chaps from Philadelphia
Was out on tour, so we challenged 'em to come along and play.
Our challenge was accepted, and one day they came around,
All ready for to play us, so we took 'em to the ground.

Joe Blazes says to me, says he, "Ole Pard, I'll tell you what,
There ain't a single shooting iron in all the blessed lot.
What do they mean a-coming 'ere, expecting for to win?
It ain't half good enough, ole pard, a jolly sight too thin."

They tossed for choice of innings, and you bet we won at that;
We all was whales on tossing, and we started for to bat.
'Twas just as well we won the toss, because, I'm bound to say,
That even if we'd lost it, we'd have batted, any way.

Wall, first of all I starts to bat, along o' Thunder Jack,
The bowler sends his ball along, I makes a mighty smack,
But, somehow, 'stead of hitting that there ball with that there bat,
I hit it with my leg. The bowler shouted "How is that?"

And that there blessed umpire started for to answer "Out",
When he saw my shooting iron – so he guessed there was a doubt;
And he'd heard as how the batsman always got the benefit,
Which plainly showed as how that blessed umpire knew a bit.

125

You'd have thought as t'other umpire would have had some common sense,
But he went and said as Jack were out, on the following pretence:
Old Jack had made a mighty swipe, and, if he'd hit the ball,
I guess we hadn't never seen that ball no more at all.

But, then, you see, he missed it, and his wickets they was downed
By the wicket-keeping chap, who said as Jack was out of ground,
And 'stead of speaking up and saying as there was a doubt,
The umpire said as Thunder Jack was very plainly out.

Then Jack he pulled his shooter out; and drew on him a bead,
And that there blessed umpire he went very dead indeed.
We shouted out "Fresh Umpire", but, somehow, no one came,
So we guessed we'd do without one, and we then resumed the game.

Wall! after that they took to bowling very nice and slow,
And, if a fielder caught a ball, he allus let it go;
So Jack and I, we slogged away as lively as could be,
Until my score was ninety-seven and Jack's was ninety-three.

Wall, we had to close our innings so's to give us time to win,
And, as they couldn't get us out, we said they might go in;
They didn't seem so anxious for to bat as you'd have thought,
But we talked to them persuasive, and convinced 'em as they ought.

We told 'em as good cricketers should sooner die than yield,
And we loaded our revolvers, and we started out to field.
We'd Rifle Bill, a deadly shot, a-fielding near the rails,
And when Bill means to shoot a chap he very rarely fails;

We'd Blazing Bob at cover point, and Mike was near the stand,
And Thunder Jack kept wicket, with his shooter in his hand,
And Lord! them Philadelphy chaps, they couldn't bat a bit;
I bowls 'em nice and easy just to tempt 'em for to hit,

But 'stead of smacking at the ball, they kept on looking back,
And seemed more interested in the ways of Thunder Jack.
One chap did hit a ball to leg, and started on a spurt,
But Rifle Bill just fetched him down, and he retired hurt.

Of course we beat 'em hollow; why, they never scored a run,
But they all admitted freely as it had been splendid fun;
So we challenged 'em to come again, and play us a return,
And, p'r'aps it may be fancy, but they didn't seem to yearn.

However, we persuaded 'em to play it out next day.
But, when the morning came, we found as they had gone away.
We've challenged other clubs since then, but one and all they states,
As, they're very, very sorry, but they have no vacant dates.
So we swept the decks completely, and we calculated that
The boss of all the cricket clubs was ours at Red Nose Flat.'

And this is what he told me – of course it mayn't be true –
But as he told the tale to me I've told the tale to you.

TEN LITTLE CADET BOYS

Ten little Cadet Boys,
  Visiting Command,
Brought with them a summer day
  Fit to beat the band.

Eleventh their Captain,
  Looking hard to see
That they all behaved themselves,
  Gorging too much tea.

Ten little Cadet Boys,
  Knocking off the shine,
Rhodes gave a catch to Drayson,
  Then there were nine.

Nine little Cadet Boys,
  Hitting with all their might,
Stone snicked the ball to wicket,
  Then there were eight.

Eight little Cadet Boys,
  Very hard had striven,
But Gray was bowled by
    Nesfield,
  Then there were seven.

Seven little Cadet Boys,
  Good at making snicks,
Lewis didn't snick at all,
  Then there were six.

Six little Cadet Boys,
  Somewhat muted, passive,
Ford put his leg in front,
  Then there were five.

Five little Cadet Boys,
  Agricultural drive,
Their Captain skyed the ball,
  Still leaving five.

Five little Cadet Boys,
  Playing grand cricket,
Bardsley hit up thirty nine,
  Didn't once snicket.

Five little Cadet Boys,
  Thought they'd make a score,
Bardsley caught by Grace of
    God,[1]
  Then there were four.

Four little Cadet Boys,
  Not so full of glee,
Pritchard didn't see the thing,
  Then there were three.

Three little Cadet Boys,
  Feeling jolly blue,
Sutton struck a ball to Marj –
  – oram, leaving two.

Two little Cadet Boys
  Forgot the ball that spun
Nesfield bowled Holmes wicket
    down,
  Then there was one.

Luff was the Cadet Boy
  Who didn't see the fun
Of hanging round all by himself,
  Then there was none.

Nesfield was the Eastco Boy
  Who, with spin and guile,
Sentenced six Cadet Boys
  To durance vile.

Ten little Cadet Boys,
  With their Captain fine,
Played attractive cricket,
  Making one one nine.

Eleven little Eastco Boys
  Determined to do well,
Of runs they added fifty five
  Before first wicket fell.

Eleven little Eastco Boys,
  Hitting hard and often,
Langley fell to wiles of Holmes,
  Leaving only ten.

Ten little Eastco Boys,
  See them shoot a line,
Drayson failed to add to score,
  Then there were nine.

Nine little Eastco Boys,
  Playing far too late,
Nesfield also took a blob,
  Then there were eight.

Eight little Eastco Boys,
    Castles crumbling down,
Couldn't add to fifty five,
    Three wickets gone.

Eight little Eastco Boys,
    Praying hard to Heaven,
Frisby left at seventy six,
    Then there were seven.

Seven little Eastco Boys
    About to cross the Styx,[2]
Thomson died an early death,
    Then there were six.

Six little Eastco Boys,
    Hitting hot and strong,
Chambers made great stacks of
    hay
While the sun shone.

Six little Eastco Boys
    With five wickets down,

Beat ten little Cadet Boys
    And Chief Hamilton.

One little Cadet Boy,
    Holmes was the name,
Took four good Eastco wickets
    At four pence a time[3]

Another little Cadet Boy,
    Bardsley, name of fame,
Fielded magnificently,
    Batted just the same.

After match was over,
    Cadets made sixty four
In another game we played,
    Half an hour each, no more.[4]

In this 'Free and Easy'
    Eastco, one five two,
Put the little Cadet Boys
    Through the hoop, right
      through!
Somerset Straggler

[1] The following entry appears in the score book:
'Cadet Bardsley c by the Grace of God b Nesfield 39.'
Our Scorer, questioned closely, stuck to her contention that Peter Gardner only
clung on to the damned thing by Divine intervention.
[2] Modern military equivalent to Charon and his boat – 194 E.
[3] Average 4.25 to be precise.
[4] 45 minutes, again to be precise.
Scorer's Notes: Thomson dropped Rhodes at 2.
                Marjoram dropped Gray at 24.
                Chambers dropped Gray at 25 and Stone at 25.
The fielding throughout, except for the lapses noted above, was of a very high
standard.